# MAD MEN
## UNBUTTONED

# A ROMP THROUGH
## 1960s AMERICA
# MAD

# MEN
## UNBUTTONED

## NATASHA VARGAS-COOPER

COLLINS DESIGN
*An Imprint of HarperCollins Publishers*

HarperCollins books may be purchased for educational, business, or sales promotional use. For information please write: Special Markets Department, HarperCollins Publishers, 10 East 53rd Street, New York, NY 10022.

FIRST EDITION

*Designed by Renato Stanisic*

Library of Congress Cataloging-in-Publication Data

Vargas-Cooper, Natasha.
  Mad men unbuttoned : a romp through 1960s America / by Natasha Vargas-Cooper.—1st ed.
    p. cm.
  ISBN 978-0-06-199100-4 (pbk.)
  1. Mad men (Television program) I. Title.
  PN1992.77.M226V37 2010
  791.45'75—dc22

                                                            2010008683

10 11 12 13 14   OV/WCT   10 9 8 7 6 5 4 3 2 1

*When history becomes too contemporary, it turns into partisan propaganda, so it seems like a good idea to start winding down this mélange of anecdotes about advertising and advertising men.*

—DRAPER DANIELS

*Lana Turner has collapsed!*

—FRANK O'HARA

**GEORGE:** *We all peel labels, sweetie; and when you get through the skin, all three layers, through the muscle, slosh aside the organs . . . them which is still sloshable—and get down to bone . . . you know what you do then?*

**HONEY:** [Terribly interested] *No!*

**GEORGE:** *When you get down to bone, you haven't got all the way yet. There's something inside the bone . . . the marrow and that's what you gotta get at.*

—EDWARD ALBEE, *WHO'S AFRAID OF VIRGINIA WOOLF?*

# CONTENTS

# INTRODUCTION

This is the shortest answer I can come up with when asked what the show *Mad Men* is about: It's about the culture clash and contradictions that occurred during the twilight of the Eisenhower era, the great societal shake-up of the 1960s, and how that pressurized time in history formed modern America, its families, its consciousness, and its consumers.

Now here's the longer answer.

In the opening credits of the show we see the silhouette of a man in a business suit enter an office with a briefcase. The sleek walls around him magically dissolve, and he plummets into a free fall. He alternately flails and goes slack as he plunges downward alongside a skyscraper. This is perhaps the easiest way to understand why *Mad Men* has become such a cultural phenomenon. Beyond its top-notch writing, complex characters, hypnotic design (really, the fusion of all these elements is the highest caliber of art, and it's so titillating to witness a renaissance in such an unlikely medium, isn't it?), there's an all-engrossing mood that permeates the show. That mixture of anxiety, instability, and tectonic cultural shifts that shook loose a whole generation feels congruent to this moment in history.

I was taught by my mentor, Murray Roston at UCLA, that every generation faces a system of inherited assumptions and urgent concerns. Discovering the ways the creative class, tastemakers, and culture producers reacted to the dominant ideas of the time—and the themes, symbols, and techniques they deployed in that moment—enriches our understanding of an entire generation. An addendum I would make to Dr. Roston's list of participants in the cultural zeitgeist would be the men (and the few women) who worked in advertising. As ad man Ed McCabe put it: "Advertising has gone from something that reflects popular culture to becoming a part of popular culture, from something that's influenced by popular entertainment to being popular entertainment."

Though the 1950s are generally regarded as a period of conformity and banality for the creative class, there likewise existed an urgent need to expose the world to some kind of emotional truth beyond the repressive sentiment of the era. Norman Mailer captured the feeling just right in a prophetic essay published in 1957:

For the first time in civilized history, perhaps for the first time in all of history, we have been forced to live with the suppressed knowledge that the smallest facets of our personality or the most minor projection of our ideas, or indeed the absence of ideas and the absence of personality could mean equally well that we might still be doomed to die as a cipher in some vast statistical operation in which our teeth would be counted, and our hair would be saved, but our death itself would be unknown, unhonored, and unremarked, a death which could not follow with dignity as a possible consequence to serious actions we had chosen, but rather a death by deus ex machina in a gas chamber or a radioactive city; and so if in the midst of civilization—that civilization founded upon the

Faustian urge to dominate nature by mastering time, mastering the links of social cause and effect—in the middle of an economic civilization founded upon the confidence that time could indeed be subjected to our will, our psyche was subjected itself to the intolerable anxiety that death being causeless, life was causeless as well, and time deprived of cause and effect had come to a stop.[1]

The bleak realities of World War II, the bomb, the camps, the annihilation of millions, according to Mailer, "presented a mirror to the human condition which blinded anyone who looked into it." The traditional values and expectations—the guilty are punished, the virtuous are rewarded, the authority of the church and state stand as legitimate—no longer held the same guarantee. Given the atrocities in Germany and Japan, some would even classify them as laughable.

*Mad Men* re-creates a discrete period of historic transition when the cultural trends and social mores that would come to dominate the second half of the decade are percolating and bubbling toward the surface. We begin to glimpse the emergent sensibility of the 1960s in the art of the late 1950s—the paintings of Mark Rothko; Frank O'Hara's poetry; California's architecture; Hollywood's juvenile delinquent movies—and in the Chicago school of advertising, which chucked out all the conventional rules of the medium in favor of a riskier, earthier style.

But this book is more than just an investigation into the history of a cultural artifact that snags a cameo on *Mad Men*. Instead, it's an attempt to re-create the cultural matrix of the moment by romping through advertising, sex, style, design, movies, literature,

---

1. All quotes from Norman Mailer, "The White Negro: Superficial Reflections on the Hipster," *Dissent* 4 (Summer 1957), 276–293.

consumption, the workplace, and politics in an attempt to understand the most dramatic American cultural shift in the twentieth century.

For this book I chose the subjects that had the greatest amount of relevance to the show. Rather than fact-check and expose anachronisms of the show (there are, indeed, a few) I wanted to focus instead on what the show got right. I also chose topics that would interest *Mad Men* fans, design junkies, history buffs, and pop culture enthusiasts. When a topic arose that I thought needed a narrative better than one I could provide, I asked someone more qualified to write about it. In these pages you will also find commentary from ad men, art critics, movie lovers, architects, authors, historians—and, of course, some very serious smokers.

**—Natasha Vargas-Cooper**
**Los Angeles**
**May 2010**

# CHARACTERS

---

**DON DRAPER:** Former creative director at Sterling Cooper and current founding partner at Sterling Cooper Draper Pryce. Raised by impoverished farmers. Former used-car salesman. Don is of the opinion that the universe is indifferent and tends to live life "like there's no tomorrow because there isn't one." Alpha male, film lover. Smokes Lucky Strikes and drinks rye with no ice. His real name is not Don Draper.

**BETTY DRAPER:** Housewife and former model. Born in the posh Philadelphia Main Line and Seven Sisters–educated (she was an anthropology major at Bryn Mawr). Betty's life experiences have been as varied as her husband's. Hobbies include smoking, horseback riding, and throwing the occasional tantrum. She dotes on the newest Draper, baby Gene, and sometimes makes an effort to parent Sally and Bobby, though during her bouts of depression and crisis leaves the mothering to her housekeeper, Carla.

**STERLING COOPER:** Fictional advertising agency. Once owned by Bertram Cooper; his sister, Alice; Roger Sterling; and Don Draper.

The ad men who work at Sterling Cooper each represent a different strain in the competing ideologies of midcentury advertising. Sterling Cooper is willingly purchased by a British advertising company, Puttnam, Powell and Lowe (likely based on real-life advertising empire Ogilvy and Mather). The British prove to be poor managers of the scrappy shop and sell it off to McCann-Erickson. A core group of employees break off to form Sterling Cooper Draper Pryce.

**BERTRAM COOPER:** A founding partner of Sterling Cooper. Eccentric; always in a bow tie and shoeless. A cajoling manager and self-made man. Art collector and Ayn Rand fan. Widower; childless.

**ROGER STERLING:** Roger's father founded Sterling Cooper in 1923 with Bertram Cooper. A World War II veteran, born into wealth. Roger embodies the self-satisfaction and sense of entitlement of the waning Eisenhower aristocracy. He is also incredibly charming.

**PEGGY OLSON:** Copywriter at Sterling Cooper Draper Pryce. Don Draper's former secretary. Brooklyn native, working-class girl, Catholic, ambitious, graduate of secretary school. Per her male co-workers, neither a "Jackie" nor a "Marilyn," but more of an Irene Dunne type. Possible prototypical feminist. Has a job, an apartment, and a sometime boyfriend; still restless.

**JOAN HARRIS (NÉE HOLLOWAY):** Office manager for Sterling Cooper Draper Pryce, former office manager at Sterling Cooper. Mother Hen to working girls; vamp to men. Former lover of Roger Sterling. Married an aspiring doctor who has decided to enlist in the army to fulfill his dream of becoming a surgeon. She once threw a vase at his head after months of mistreatment.

**PETE CAMPBELL:** Head of accounts at Sterling Cooper Draper Pryce; former accounts manager at Sterling Cooper. A Dartmouth man and, by way of his mother, descendant of New York royalty (Pete is occasionally known to introduce himself to the rich and powerful as "Peter Dykeman Campbell"). Simultaneously whining and conniving, Pete dreams of having his name on an agency masthead. He enjoys doing the Charleston with his wife, Trudy, eating cereal in his pajamas, and wolfishly pursuing au pairs and would-be models.

**RACHEL MENKEN:** Don's onetime Jewess lover. Owner of Menken's department store. Likely to be the woman who came closest, besides Betty, to making Don Draper fall in love with her.

**PAUL KINSEY:** Copywriter at Sterling Cooper. Self-identified bearded rebel in advertising. Aspiring novelist; pretentious but harmless. Princeton graduate, all-male a cappella enthusiast.

**SALVATORE ROMANO:** Former art director at Sterling Cooper. Lone Italian in a nest of WASPs. Married to the devoted (and neglected) Kitty, but caught by Don in a same-sex tryst. Draper's advice to Sal? "Limit your exposure," which he does, with mixed results.

**BOBBIE BARRETT:** Don Draper's former high-powered mistress. Wife and manager to trash-talking comedian Jimmy Barrett (a spokesman for Sterling Cooper's client Utz Potato Chips). Brassy, always with a cigarette holder and a counteroffer. Bobbie bests Don when it comes to being forward. It is she who paws Don in the front seat of his car. But Don's rough with Bobbie. In their final tryst, Don takes Bobbie's nylons, ties her to the bed, and then leaves her. Though she doesn't flinch when she sees him again.

**KEN COSGROVE:** Head of accounts at Sterling Cooper. Skilled with clients. Published a short story in *Atlantic Monthly,* much to the chagrin and envy of his coworkers. Expert skirt chaser.

**HARRY CRANE:** Head of the Television Department at Sterling Cooper Draper Pryce. Formerly self-appointed head of media at Sterling Cooper. New father.

**HERMAN "DUCK" PHILLIPS:** Former head of accounts at Sterling Cooper. Convinces his onetime employer Puttnam, Powell and Lowe to buy out Sterling Cooper. Often overreaching and dismissive of Don's talents. However, Duck is not impervious to advertising trends nor to the talents of Pete Campbell and Peggy Olson. Makes dubious personal and business decisions.

**JANE STERLING:** Don Draper's twentysomething secretary turned Roger Sterling's replacement wife. College grad and self-styled naughty girl who enjoys the attention of Sterling Cooper's male employees. Writes poems about Roger; is easily intoxicated and hysterical. Does not understand why she is disliked by others.

**CARLA:** The Drapers' black housekeeper and de facto nanny.

**LANE PRYCE:** Puttnam, Powell and Lowe's appointed accounts manager at Sterling Cooper; founding partner of Sterling Cooper Draper Pryce. Droll, British, efficient bean counter.

**MIDGE DANIELS:** The first of Don Draper's mistresses we are introduced to. Bohemian, Greenwich Village dweller, openly promiscuous, and independent, she tells Don, "You know the rules: I don't make plans, and I don't make breakfast." Makes her scratch illustrating greeting cards. Enjoys Miles Davis, smoking weed, and relishes worldly discussions. Pals around with scruffy Beats who employ the word *bourgeois* when it comes to things like love.

**SALLY DRAPER:** Prepubescent daughter of Betty and Don. Daddy's girl.

**CAROL MCCARDY:** Joan's former roommate and closet lesbian.

**SUZANNE FARRELL:** Don's most recent extramarital affair. Sally Draper's bright-eyed schoolteacher. Alludes to having bedded more than one suburban father. Bakes date nut bread.

**FRANCINE HANSON:** Ossining housewife, friend of Betty, pregnant smoker. Francine introduces Betty to the Junior League and provides opportunity and encouragement for her affair with political operative Henry Francis. Always up for neighborhood gossip in the Draper kitchen.

**HELEN BISHOP:** Attractive divorcée on the Drapers' block. Mother of two, Kennedy campaign volunteer, and jewelry counter clerk. Unpopular with the other mothers.

# MADMEN
## UNBUTTONED

# 1

## THE ADS AND THE MEN
## WHO MADE THEM

Marlboro Red
or Longhorn 100's—
you get a lot to like.

# Come to where the flavor is. Come to Marlboro Country.

# LEO BURNETT: THE BOY WHO THE EARTH TALKS TO

For its October 12, 1962, cover, *Time* magazine created an illustrated collage that pasted oranges alongside cigarettes, the Kool-Aid man, the Manhattan skyline, cotton panties, and the Kellogg's Cornflakes rooster, with the hair dye slogan "Does she, or doesn't she?" across its width. Embedded alongside images of logos and supermarket goods are the faces of a dozen men. White, unsmiling, conservative-looking men who could have easily blended in at a place like IBM or the FBI. But this square-looking cadre were the vanguard of a creative revolution. So while the inscrutable faces of Leo Burnett, David Ogilvy, and Bill Bernbach appeared seemingly interchangeable, each represented a unique, and at times warring, ideological school of advertising that permanently altered the way Americans interacted with their marketplace.

Based on his approach and espoused beliefs about what makes advertising good, Don Draper would be (or is) a disciple of Leo Burnett's Chicago School of advertising: homespun, straightforward, familiar.

For Burnett, image trumped the copy. The photography or illustration for an ad needed to be evocative so it could easily trigger consumers' emotions and circumvent their initial prejudices.

Rather than using ad space to extol the virtues of a product (as David Ogilvy did so elegantly), or make folks chuckle (like Bill Bernbach did), Burnett wanted to reflect the consumers' basic desires and beliefs back to them by speaking their language. Burnett wanted to craft a lingua franca in advertising through visuals to which Americans would instinctually respond.[1]

In Burnett's words, the visuals themselves needed to capture "the inherent drama of everyday life." Burnett's 1945 American Meat Institute ad campaign exemplified this ideal.

At the time it was considered vulgar to show uncooked meat in advertisements. But Burnett thought the symbolic power of raw meat was too rich to ignore. "We convinced ourselves that the image of meat should be a virile one, best expressed in red meat," Burnett said of the campaign. He produced full-page ads with

1. History would ultimately prove Burnett right, as television advertisements, a visually dominant medium, became the lifeblood of American consumption instead of print advertising. "Television," Burnett said in 1940, "is the strongest drug we've ever had to dish out."

thick chops of raw, red meat against a bright red background. "Red against red was a trick," Burnett explained. "It was a natural thing to do. It just intensified the concept and the virility and everything else we were trying to express. . . . This was inherent drama in its purest form."[2]

Burnett was born to a middle-class family in Michigan at the turn of the century. He worked as a police reporter for the *Peoria Journal* for a few years, then went over to Cadillac to edit its in-house magazine.[3] In 1919 he became advertising manager for the Michigan Cadillac store. Roughly twenty years later, Burnett borrowed $50,000 and founded his own ad agency based in Chicago.[4] The Midwestern location was not an accident. Burnett believed the tastes of heartland folk accurately encompassed American sensibilities writ large; if you wanted to sell to the American public, you needed an "earthy vernacular" instead of clever wordplay or snobbery.

"We try to be—which I think typifies the Chicago school of advertising, if there is one, and I think there is one—we try to be more straightforward without being flatfooted," Leo told an interviewer. "We try to be warm without being mawkish."[5]

But the heartland was not buzzing with copywriters. So Burnett recruited and heavily mentored a hand-selected few; those who came out of the Chicago shop were considered Leo's disciples, and they treated his ethos like gospel.

---

2. Denis Higgins, *The Art of Writing Advertising: Conversations with Masters of the Craft* (New York: McGraw-Hill, 2003), 46. It's worth noting that Chicago is the city of slaughterhouses.

3. Must I remind you what Don Draper ran before he went to Sterling Cooper? Okay, hint: a car dealership.

4. Burnett's father was a grocer and created his store's own advertising, so legend goes. Burnett would run his father's ads over to the newspaper, and that's what sparked his interest in working for the paper. Images such as cowboys smoking and effervescent teens drinking soda became the language of commerce, each image connoting specific archetypal traits of youth, masculinity, or independence, etc.

5. Denis Higgins, *The Art of Writing Advertising*, 44.

The word *brand* is bandied about so often—from advertising to politics to social media strategies—that it's difficult to believe that it was at one point a revolutionary concept. Burnett wanted a "brand picture engraved on the customer's consciousness." You hear this philosophy of branding when Don admonishes Peggy's "sex sells," when she turns in lackluster copy.

Don says to Peggy, "Just so you know, the people who talk that way think monkeys can do this. They take all this monkey crap and just stick it in a briefcase, completely unaware that their success depends on something more than a shoeshine. *You* are the product. You, *feeling* something—that's what sells."[6]

Burnett created brand identity for his clients with character logos. A good-humored giant who kept watch over the harvest, an energetic tiger bounding out into the day, a cherubic little house pet made of dough—and of course, a rugged cowboy stoically smoking a cigarette. Burnett was responsible for the Jolly Green Giant, Tony the Tiger, the Pillsbury Doughboy, and most (in)famously, the Marlboro Man.

As Madison Avenue shops such as McCann and J. Walter Thompson snapped up as many megaclients as they could and opened up shops overseas, Burnett kept his company successful with a small shop and a short list of loyal clients. This difference in management style played itself out in the American Airlines fiasco between Don and Duck Phillips in Season Two. Duck convinces Roger and Bert to ditch the midlevel Mohawk Airlines in order to woo American Airlines (the switch, Duck argued, could result in exchanging a one-million-dollar account for a seven-million-dollar account). "We already have an airline," Don protested, "a

6. "Stop writing for other writers." This is the advice Don gives Paul Kinsey after hearing him rattle off a number of Indian-related puns for the Mohawk Airline account in the same episode ("For Those Who Think Young"). This critique was often leveled at ad legend Bill Bernbach and other ad men of the era; they were trying too hard to impress one another rather than the consumer.

good client who trusts us, who likes our work, who pays their bill on time. They don't deserve to be thrown out the door for a wink from American."

In a 1967 speech to his company, Burnett shared Don's sentiment:

"Somewhere along the line, after I am finally off the premises, you—or your successors—may want to take my name off the premises, too. You may want to call yourselves 'Twain, Rogers, Sawyer, and Finn, Incorporated' or 'Ajax Advertising' or something. That will certainly be okay with me—if it's good for you. But let me tell you when I might demand that you take my name off the door: . . . When you stoop to convenient expediency and rationalize yourselves into acts of opportunism—for the sake of a fast buck."[7]

The Leo Burnett Company still exists today as one of the largest ad agencies in the country. Its clients include McDonald's, Coca-Cola, Walt Disney, Marlboro, Maytag, Kellogg's, Tampax, Nintendo, Philips, Samsung, Visa, Wrigley's, Hallmark, Allstate Insurance, and Procter & Gamble. It has ninety-seven offices in eighty-four countries.

Leo Burnett proved a morally ambiguous hypothesis to be true: Visual form is more persuasive than carefully reasoned argument.

---

7. Leo Burnett, "When to Take My Name Off the Door," speech given December 1, 1967.

# DRAPER DANIELS
# STRAINS OUT THE SISSY TASTE

Draper Daniels sat in the royal court of advertising during its golden reign on Madison Avenue. He was anointed one of the best copywriters in the biz by his mentor, Leo Burnett, and went on to do work at the most influential agencies—including the government—until his death in 1983.

Daniels got his start in the influence business selling Vicks VapoRub door-to-door in the South. With a master's degree in education from Syracuse University, he was offered a job at the public school where his mother taught. He turned it down for Vicks Chemical Company training that offered writers a crack at New York copywriting if they spent a year in the field pitching products on customers' doorsteps.[1] This gave Daniels the practical education in what ordinary folks respond to and enabled him to flourish under men like Burnett.

In his autobiography *Giants, Pigmies and Other Advertising People*, Daniels wrote, "When I was fourteen, I had been shown New York in a confusion of taxicabs, subways, and buses, and had made up my mind never to live there if I could help it. Obviously, I hadn't been able to help it, so there I was, alone, feeling as if I had tried to swallow a tennis ball and it had stuck about halfway."[2]

Daniels managed to acclimate quickly (after some rounds of tennis with friends in Brooklyn) and eventually got hired at Young & Rubicam, which in the 1940s had a first-rate roster that included

---

1. Draper Daniels, *Giants, Pigmies, and Other Advertising People* (Chicago: Crain Communications, 1974), 3. "A salesman," he wrote, "traveling, or otherwise, was the last thing in the world I wanted to be, but the 'plus expenses and a car [offer]' shattered any sales resistance."

2. Ibid., 4.

General Foods, Met Life, American Tobacco (Lucky Strike), and Windex.[3] Daniels worked in a Paul Kinsey capacity—writing paragraphs about cigarettes, sewing machines, and gasoline. After three years he was offered a copy chief position in Chicago with McCann-Erickson.[4]

Daniels, by his own admission, played tough with some big accounts while at McCann, and some of the speeches he gave clients could have been tossed at a stubborn Sterling Cooper client. Here is Daniels's account of a spanking he gave Purity Bakeries (they billed more than a million dollars with McCann): "You seem to think we're here to sell you some advertising and that you're here to buy some advertising. As long as you have that idea you're never going to get anything worthwhile from any agency. . . . Now maybe we didn't listen hard enough or you didn't explain your problems as clearly as you thought you did. That doesn't matter. What does matter is that we do it right the second time. Would you mind giving us the message again?"[5]

Leo Burnett eventually poached Daniels to be the head of his creative department in 1954. Daniels was put on a huge account to solve a problem for a cigarette company: How to get the public to feel safe about smoking. Daniels decided to focus on the company's specialty brand of filtered cigarettes, which had up until 1957 been marketed entirely toward women. The brand was called Marlboro.

Daniels pitched selling the brand to men. "If we showed big

---

3. Young & Rubicam was the premier ad agency of the 1940s. During the infamous Heineken-fueled dinner party at the Drapers' ("A Night to Remember"), Roger and Don rub shoulders with an ad man who worked at Young & Rubicam. He was treated like a very big deal. Per Daniels, the dream job for young copywriters was a gig at Y&R: "Young & Rubicam was heaven, or the next door to it, and God's name was Rubicam."

4. McCann has made several appearances in the show—they are the bad guys who send Don golf clubs, use Betty as a bargaining chip in the Coca-Cola ad, and eventually buy Sterling Cooper from PPL.

5. Daniels, *Giants*, 165.

rugged men puffing Marlboros, we would automatically say it had big, rugged real flavor instead of a strained-out sissy taste."[6]

From 10:00 A.M. on a Saturday to 3:00 P.M. Sunday, Daniels's team:

---

- ✖ Redesigned the package: Made the stripes blood red and bold instead of thin and pinkish. Increased the size and thickness of the *M* by capitalizing it.
- ✖ Found the cowboy: He came from a photo spread *Life* magazine had done four years prior.
- ✖ Wrote the copy headline: "The filter that delivers the goods on flavor."
- ✖ Made their argument: The masculine copy never referred to the filter, just the bold taste men could enjoy.[7]

---

Like Don Draper, Draper Daniels was supernaturally good at his work—but unlike Don, he was also a pretty open fellow who quickly kicked booze, adored his wife (she was COO of an agency Draper's merged with), and even wrote a dishy book about himself and his coworkers.

Oh, and as you may already know, per Daniels, "Philip Morris liked the ad."

---

6. Ibid., 244. From all the accounts I've read about the Marlboro campaign, every one from the art director to the mailroom clerk has taken credit for the idea of virile men smoking and looking tough. As you can see so often in the show, these ideas are rarely created in a vacuum. So it's entirely possible that every one has a little bit of credit. But the Marlboro campaign has ultimately been regarded as Burnett's brainchild.

7. Ibid., 241.

# BE MANLY, GET LUCKY: LUCKY STRIKE

The Lucky Strike executives sitting impatiently in the Sterling Cooper conference room are spooked. They can no longer use doctors and other medical authority figures to endorse cigarettes because of the mounting studies linking cigarettes and cancer. "This is the greatest advertising opportunity since the invention of cereal," Don tells the anxious tobacco men. "We have six identical companies making six identical products." What differentiated the Lucky Strike brand? It's toasted! Don explains. "Everyone else's tobacco is poisonous. Lucky Strike's is toasted."

Even though all tobacco is toasted before being made into cig-arettes, the print and TV campaign of the 1940s showed Lucky Strike tobacco farmers scoring the highest price at auction because of their artisan toasting style. The idea behind Don's pitch was to neutralize health concerns by completely skirting them. The goal, per Don's logic, was to reassure the customer that everything they were doing, including smoking that Lucky, was okay.[1]

After decades of relying on their stand-by slogan, Lucky Strike switched to an ad campaign of Manly Men Doing Manly Things in 1961. Based on the smash success of the iconic Marlboro campaign, which overcame health fears by ignoring them and instead revital-ized its brand by giving its smokes a distinctly masculine personal-ity, Lucky Strike began to mimic the Marlboro campaign.[2] Instead of winsome cowboys, though, they featured all sorts of men in its

---

1. Just a fun aside about Don's brand loyalty to Lucky Strike: Leo Burnett was once asked why he smoked Marlboro cigarettes. Burnett responded: "In my book there is no taste or aroma quite like bread and butter."

2. The Marlboro Man is commonly known as the "campaign of the century." Not only was the ad emblematic of the new style of advertising—evocative, brand-focused—but it also completely reinvented a product based solely on the quality of its advertising. Even David Ogilvy was impressed. Speaking a few months after the campaign began, he said, "[Burnett] took some risks which few advertisers would take. Most notably, they seem to have decided that Marlboro should have an exclusively male personality. What a brave decision!"

Light up
a Lucky...
it's light-up
time!

LUCKY
STRIKE
CIGARETTES
L.S./M.F.T.

"IT'S
TOASTED"
to taste
better!

**WHAT A DAY** ... what a game ... what a cigarette! Why is a Lucky so much a part of moments like this? It's the fact that Luckies *taste* better ... rich, mellow, thoroughly pleasant. Luckies taste better, first of all, because Lucky Strike means fine tobacco. Then, this tobacco is *toasted*. *"It's Toasted"* to taste even better ... cleaner, fresher, smoother. So, light up a Lucky, the better-tasting cigarette.

# LUCKIES TASTE BETTER - *Cleaner, Fresher, Smoother!*

ads: hunters, farmers, fishermen, playboys, men in fast cars—men of any sort as long as they were worthy of some hard-won stubble. Nevertheless, by this time Marlboro was synonymous with plaintive masculinity.

"Even then, my mind screamed MARLBORO!" Mark Duffy, vice president and associate creative director of a New York–based firm told me in a 2009 interview when I showed him the 1960s Lucky Strike ad series. "I'm sure executives at Lucky Strike's parent company, American Tobacco Company, stewed at the time, as they watched Marlboro's brilliant strategy turn a filtered, feminine cigarette into the choice for rugged men. This apparent piggybacking on an established strategy probably just sold more Marlboro cases."

# WESTERN UNION:
# WHAT MAKES A GREAT AD?[1] BY TIM SIEDELL

Great ads are simple.[2]

The talented people who work in advertising agencies know this. But, God help them, they often can't help themselves. A talented wordsmith may want to squeeze in just one more clever line. The art director may want to add just one more stylistic flourish. And that's just in the creative department. The account executive might want to hedge his bets and work in some more sales copy about a second or third product line in order to please his client. And all bets are off if the client gets down into the trenches. Or (shudder) the client's spouse.

And that's why there are so few great ads.

This one is. Throw out the fact it's selling telegrams. Ignore the dated headline typeface. Don't worry, modern reader, about the lack of a website address for more information. This would be a great ad in 1983, 2003, or today.

The crafters of this ad understood human nature. Tell us to ignore something, and we won't be able to. Snap. Which is the entire idea of the ad. Not just the idea of a clever copywriter/art director team, mind you. Those are a dime a dozen. No, it's the very essence of a Western Union telegram. It's not just a powerful idea; it's a *relevant* idea. And those kinds of ideas are worth their weight in gold.

Now, notice the craft of the art director. The layout forces you to quickly glance at the yellow telegram, but the bold typeface and dramatic white space pulls your eye upward to the headline. You've already noticed that there is small type in the telegram and, good grief, there's no way you're not going to read that copy.

---

1. Entry by Tim Siedell, the creative director of Fuse Industries. He knows craft.

2. This ad was created by Doyle Dane Bernbach.

# Ignore it

IGNORE A TELEGRAM?  YOU CAN'T. NO ONE EVER IGNORED A TELEGRAM. YOUR TELEGRAM ALWAYS COMPELS IMMEDIATE ATTENTION — AND IMMEDIATE RESPONSE.

TO BE SURE TO GET ACTION, SEND A TELEGRAM.

Now, notice the craft of the copywriter. The copy gets right to the point. Because, again, that's the idea of a telegram. This is no time for fluffy copy or clever wordplay. And while the writer no doubt could craft a double entendre that would make your head spin and smile in admiration, he or she should be commended for showing masterful restraint here.

Now, notice the craft of the creative director. A powerful creative hand helped guide this ad through final approval, no doubt. See how there are no superfluous elements? No background texture. No colors to distract from the yellow telegram. The copy is contained in the telegram. There's not even a need for a logo, as the client's name is proudly displayed on the telegram itself. There's not a single detail here that's not needed (or organically part of a Western Union telegram). Everything has been stripped away so the focus is on the idea itself.

A single powerful, relevant idea simply executed. It sounds easy. It's not. Whether you worked in advertising in 1963 or today.

# "SIGMUND" CAMPBELL:
# THE SMOKER'S DEATH WISH

Pete Campbell shows his sharp-elbow tendencies when he salvages a discarded psychological report conducted for the Lucky Strike account from Don's trash can. Sterling Cooper's straight-out-of-Vienna consulting psychologist recommends Lucky Strike embrace the danger of smoking in its advertisements because *all* consumers supposedly carry within them a secret "death wish."

The death wish is fundamental Freud. He posited that men and women harbored a counterintuitive drive toward self-destruction to counterbalance our will to live. Freud argued, because death is so terrifying and beyond our comprehension, we are subliminally attracted to it. The more repressive a society, the stronger that attraction becomes. So according to the fräulein shrink, who authored the trashed report, Lucky Strike should tout its dangerous qualities to the public and appeal directly to its death drive.

Don is downright offended at the suggestion whereas Pete is intrigued. What may have piqued Pete's interest, more than his own masochistic streak, was the manipulative effect psychology could play in cigarette advertising. Rather than influence consumers about how they should feel about a product, a nonacademic endeavor according to Don, research psychology could allow an ad agency to quickly meet the whims and tastes of a consumer; Sterling Cooper would be able to craft a campaign with perfect flexibility.

When Don stumbles during the pitch, Pete offers up the "death wish" and a glib "you're-going-to-die-anyway-so-light-'em-up" slogan. The cigarette men are appalled.

There is one psychological concept that Pete seems not to have mastered: denial.

# DAVID OGILVY: **FOR THE SNOB IN YOU**

A specter is haunting Sterling Cooper—David Ogilvy.[1]

There is the country mouse ethos of Conrad Hilton; the earthy vernacular of Leo Burnett; the cheeky humor of Bill Bernbach. And there's David Ogilvy, whose advertising philosophy is represented by the limey bosses of Puttnam, Powell and Lowe: austere, logical, and unabashedly aristocratic.[2]

Ogilvy was born in London in 1911, and though he spent most of his adulthood in the States, he never dropped the affectations of a dustily well-bred English snob (complete with a tweed jacket and pipe).

If the question on Madison Avenue was how to best sell products to Americans, Ogilvy's answer was: Find out what they wanted and up-sell them—no matter how rich they were. Ogilvy knew his audience, through painstaking research, and pandered to its fantasies. The Ogilvy holy trinity follows:

*Research:* Ogilvy spent three years as a researcher for George Gallup's Audience Research Group. He manned more than four hundred opinion polls and studies. In his book *Ogilvy on Advertising,* he wrote: "You don't stand a tinker's chance of producing successful advertising unless you start by doing your homework. I have always found this extremely tedious, but there is no substitute for it." If you refuse to poll the people you are trying to sell cars or tailored shirts to, you would, according to Ogilvy, quickly

---

1. Pete threatens to go over to Ogilvy when he feels passed over at Sterling Cooper. Additionally, the young millionaire Ho-Ho, who dreams of bringing the Basque sport jai alai to the States, tells Don over dinner that he should be thankful for his business because he could have "taken this over to Ogilvy." When Roger begins to feel his company slip from under him, he bristles that Don is like Sterling Cooper's Ogilvy.

2. In 1989 Ogilvy's own ad company was purchased in a hostile takeover by WPP, a British holding company. Sir Martin Sorrell, the holding company's CEO, was, in Ogilvy's words, an "odious little shit" and he promised to never work for him again.

plummet down "what my brother Francis called 'the slippery surface of irrelevant brilliance.' "[3]

*Status:* No matter how mundane a product, Ogilvy believed more people would buy it if it was given elevated (even if it was arbitrary) distinction. Take the Hathaway shirt campaign. In 1950 C. F. Hathaway sold its middle-quality shirts to about 450 retailers. By 1962 Hathaway was selling its line to more than 2,500 retailers nationwide. This feat was almost entirely accomplished by Ogilvy's print campaign, which ran only in the *New Yorker,* the *New York Times,* and *Sports Illustrated.* Deposed White Russian baron and part-time model George Wrangell was featured in all the ads. Wrangell, a slight man of short stature, had salt-and-pepper hair and a pencil mustache. To add an air of distinction, Ogilvy slapped an eye patch on him. The headline read, "To my son Benjamin I leave—one million dollars and all my Hathaway shirts."[4]

*Copy:* The text had to argue the virtue of the product: no puns, nothing funny, no analogies, and sentences should run under twelve words.

Ogilvy was responsible for General Foods, Bristol-Myers, Campbell Soup, Schweppes, Lever Brothers, Shell, Rolls-Royce, and—most famously—a copy-heavy ad for Mercedes-Benz that consisted of twelve paragraphs arguing the superiority of its engine. Mercedes sales went from 10,000 cars a year to 40,000 cars a year. The trick was that Ogilvy made buying high-end products seem like a sensible use of one's money. Robert Glatzer sums up Ogilvy's impact on advertising precisely: "He was able to add an element of

---

3. David Ogilvy, *Ogilvy on Advertising* (New York: Crown, 1983), 11–12.

4. In his 1963 book, *Confessions of an Ad Man,* Ogilvy wrote: "H. L. Mencken once said that nobody ever went broke underestimating the taste of the American public. That is not true. I have come to believe that it pays to make all your layouts project a feeling of good taste, provided that you do it unobtrusively. An ugly layout suggests an ugly product. There are very few products which do not benefit from being given a first-class ticket through life."

Hathaway reveals the truth about men who wear drip-dry shirts

fiction to his clients' products, to create fantasies for consumers to associate with them, that seemed to make his client's products more desirable than their competitors'. And the austerity of his writing made the fantasies more believable. One could identify much more closely with the man in the Hathaway shirt than with a man in an Arrow shirt."[5]

David Ogilvy made a lot of money off David Ogilvy. His books on advertising have become doctrine to a generation of ad men and entrepreneurs. He is constantly cited for bringing a European sensibility to American advertisers. He was a craftsman but has also been referred to as a traitor to the creative field of advertising because he evangelized the dos and don'ts of advertising, which could stifle creativity, but also helped separate the hucksters from the professionals. Ogilvy, in essence, was the businessman's creative man.

5. Robert Glatzer, *The New Advertising: The Great Campaigns from Avis to Volkswagen* (New York: Citadel Press, 1970), 55.

# REDESIGNING MENKEN'S: MATRIARCHS OF THE SALES FLOOR

To attract a new clientele to her Fifth Avenue department store, Sterling Cooper's research team offers Rachel Menken these solutions: spacious shopping floors with a "conspicuous lack of clutter," Spartan window displays, and a personal shopping service.

The department store, perhaps more than any other structure, reflected the palimpsest of American culture. For the first time people of modest means could access the pleasure and beauty usually reserved for elites. The department store set a lifestyle standard and codified our modern identity as consumers.

Nineteenth-century markets and general stores were overstuffed with merchandise. Products poured out of barrels or were haphazardly piled on top of one another in crates. Consumer goods were shelved rather than displayed. In the midcentury, space became luxury because it implied scarcity. When a void is created around an object it commands a single focus and creates a direct dialogue with the customer. One dress elevated on display speaks to women more forcefully than twenty on a rack.

The goal was to create a museumlike atmosphere where cuff links and washing machines could be regarded as more than just commodities; they could exist as objects to be admired—and who doesn't want to own admirable things?

A personal shopper could help a woman navigate the new territory of chic fashion and new gadgets (think of all those gleaming new appliances!). The department store sales floor was a place of power for women. A personal shopper served as a tastemaker for the modern woman: from kitten heels to curtains, a saleswoman could define an entire lifestyle. If a lady shopper decided to forgo the matriarchs of the sales floor, she could wander independently

Shoppers at Bonwit Teller's linen counter, circa 1950s.

and purchase items based solely on her preferences (and income, of course).

The department store was considered the grand redeemer of monotonous mass production because it embraced twentieth-century notions of high culture. The store Rachel envisioned was one that embodied the modern virtues of a new era rather than a discount.

## Do you think the Volkswagen is homely?

The Volkswagen was designed from the inside out.

Every line is a result of function. The snub nose cuts down wind resistance. The body lines hug the interior workings. Nothing protrudes.

One Briton called the Volkswagen "a marvelous economy of design."

An American owner put it differently. "It's funny," he said, "how she grows on you. At first you think she's the homeliest thing you ever saw. But pretty soon you get to love her shape. And after awhile, no other car looks right."

The VW defies obsolescence. You can hardly tell the doughty shape of a 1950 model from a '61. To suggest altering it is heresy to owners. (Would you change the perfect form of an egg?)

But we are continually making changes you cannot see. Example: a new anti-sway bar eliminates sway on curves. Over a hundred such changes since 1950, but never in the basic design.

Is the Volkswagen homely? It depends on how you look at it (and how long).

# WEST GERMANY V. DETROIT:
# THE VOLKSWAGEN CAMPAIGN

It was a car invented by the Nazis, repackaged by a Jewish-owned advertising agency, and sold as an underdog option to the bloated cars out of Detroit. It became a symbol of consumer counterculture. It was ugly, it was cramped, and it was named after a bug.

"But we learned that Hitler's 'people's car' had a lot going for it," art designer George Lois wrote after returning from Volkswagen's factory in Wolfsburg, Germany, with copywriter Julian Koenig. "Julian saw it as a dumb, honest, little car—but a marketing enigma. New York was our biggest market for our new account, and that's what made it so tough."[1] They had visited VW on assignment for Doyle Dane Bernbach, creators of the iconic Western Union ad.

If David Ogilvy exploited the class aspirations of consumers to get them to spend money, and Leo Burnett's campaigns spoke in a lingua franca so that products reflected American sensibilities, then Bill Bernbach's greatest—some hail as *the* greatest—contribution to advertising's creative revolution was counterintuitive marketing. Bernbach took the perceived disadvantages of a product and turned them into their most desirable aspect. With the Beetle, Bernbach positioned the little car as a revolt against American excess. The vulgar Detroit cars were oversize, larded with unnecessary accents that increased their prices (fins, chrome, etc.), and every few years you would have to buy another to stay current.

Koenig's copy acknowledged the Beetle was homely, squat, and had been derisively referred to as a lemon, but argued that the VW's lack of flare was because German car inspectors—3,389 to be

---

1. George Lois, *George, Be Careful: A Greek Florist's Kid in the Roughhouse World of Advertising* (New York: Saturday Review Press, 1972), 59.

exact—spent more time perfecting an efficient product than adding frippery to a car that would only depreciate over time.

Thanks almost entirely to the Bernbach campaign, sales went up to a staggering 500,000 a year.

Bernbach's (and his disciples') ability to challenge consumers' beliefs about a product while simultaneously enticing them to buy it distinguishes him as one of the most influential forces of modern advertising.

"Now I'm not talking about tricking people," Bernbach said. "If you get attention by a trick, how can people like you for it? For instance, you are not right if, in your ad, you stand a man on his head just to get attention. But you are right to have him on his head to show how your product keeps things from falling out of his pockets."[2]

Lois summed up the legendary campaign this way: "We sold the Nazi car in a Jewish town by junking all the rules of car advertising. It could have only happened at Bill Bernbach's agency."[3]

2. Ibid., 17.

3. Ibid., 61.

# THE PROMISCUOUS MINGLING OF ART AND COPY: JULIAN KOENIG AND GEORGE LOIS

Salvatore Romano is segregated from his cohorts in Sterling Cooper's creative department because he's an art guy. The old-school idea was: Advertising is a written medium. The most successful ad, it was believed, had the most convincing argument (or a really great headline). Up until the mid-1960s the industry's creative powers were all copywriters while art directors, such as Sal, were considered subordinate "layout men."

That idea was demolished when copywriter Julian Koenig and art director George Lois were put together under Bill Bernbach's supervision at Doyle Dane Bernbach.[1] "There was an unprecedented level of creative collaboration," George Lois wrote in his autobiography. "Art directors would sometimes have a hand in creating copy and writers would often have hand in layout . . . it was thrilling." It turned out that art and copy were in a veritable fury to communicate and were able to create ads that fulfilled the full potential of their creative talents.[2]

After the success of the Volkswagen campaign, Koenig and Lois broke off and started their own company (Papert, Koenig, Lois), and it was the first time an art director's name was on the masthead.[3] Several ad men followed their lead and art/copy teams became a hot trend on the Avenue. Presumably, this is why Duck tells Roger that

---

1. Lois is perhaps best known now as the art director for *Esquire* magazine's most iconic covers in the late 1960s: Andy Warhol drowning in a can of tomato soup; Muhammad Ali posed as Saint Sebastian with arrows jutting out from his flesh; and actress Virna Lisi shaving her face for the cover story "The Masculinization of the American Woman." He also coined the phrase "I want my MTV."

2. When Kurt and Smitty interview at Sterling Cooper and show Don Draper their portfolio, Don remarks, "Book's good. By the way, it has Julian Koenig's fingerprints all over it."

3. Koenig designed the Timex torture test commercials, which featured the tagline "Timex: It takes a licking and keeps on ticking." Koenig also created the campaign for Earth Day in 1969.

| Papert | Koenig | Lois |

Sterling Cooper should hire "one of those teams—the writer and the artist together? Clients keep bringing it up." Enter Kurt and Smitty, with their super zeitgeist-y sensibilities.

PKL was also very hip, according to Lois. "The joint was un-befouled by mannerism—and nothing could stop us. I was in love with my loosey-goosey paradise. We worked late because it was painful to leave its carefree atmosphere, where everyone was always so wide awake."[4]

But of course, such large egos on one masthead can be an organizational challenge. Lois left in 1967 to start his own company. Lois and Koenig have been in a feud over their work for the past forty years. Koenig told *This American Life* contributing editor Sarah Koenig, his daughter, in 2009 that "George is a talented storyteller with a vivid imagination. The only thing that could exceed it would be the truth."

4. George Lois, *George, Be Careful: A Greek Florist's Kid in the Roughhouse World of Advertising* (New York:, Saturday Review Press, 1972), 85.

# POLAROID: MORE POWERFUL THAN MEMORY ALONE

The challenge, presented by the Eastman family to the creative team at Sterling Cooper, is to take a clunky Kodak gadget, a slide projector, and make it exciting. "Technology," Don tells the men from Kodak, "is a glittering lure, but there's the rare occasion where the public can be engaged on a level beyond flash." Don cuts the lights, the slide projector flickers on the wall, and he begins to court the room's sense of sentimentality with snapshots from the Draper family's photo album: Sally and Don napping on the couch surrounded by toys and torn-up Christmas wrapping paper; Bobby in a red wagon being pulled down the sidewalk by his sister; Don, his eyes closed, resting his cheek on top of Betty's swollen baby belly; a candid shot of Betty and Don kissing at a New Year's Eve party.

"Nostalgia," Don says over his family slide show, "literally means 'the pain from an old wound.' It's a twinge in your heart far more powerful than memory alone. This device isn't a spaceship, it's a time machine. It goes backwards, forwards . . . it takes us to a place where we ache to go again. It's not called 'the wheel,' it's called 'the carousel.' It lets us travel the way a child travels—around and around, and back home again, to a place where we *know* we are loved."

Delicate, potent, and beyond flash, Don's pitch to Kodak is high art; it fulfills the promise of the advertising medium as instant and emotional. It was likely inspired by the beloved Polaroid campaign of the midsixties by Doyle Dane Bernbach. "Everybody says, 'Well, Polaroid. How can you miss? It's a natural for advertising. All you have to do is show it,'" remarked an art director for DDB. "They forget that BBDO had the Polaroid account for five years,

# It's like opening a present.

Shown: Model 100, under $150, including flash.

Polaroid
Color Pack
Cameras
start at
under '60.

and it looked like shit." The ads were cheap-looking and marketed the bulky camera with text-heavy spreads that explained the new technology of "instant photographs."

The team at DDB decided to focus on the pictures instead of the process. They hired photographer Howard Zieff to shoot a series of homespun pictures that had the feel of a candid shot of typical but quintessential American life: barefoot kids catching toads, family dinners in messy kitchens, daughters giving living room dance recitals. To best communicate the simplicity of the product, the copywriters used only one sentence: "It's like opening a present."

According to Robert Glatzer, author of *The New Advertising,* Polaroid's television ads perfected the campaign: "Some of them have brought viewers to tears by their portrayal of sentimental, touching moments, which is rather an accomplishment in sixty seconds of commercial time. It is even possible to say that these commercials, on occasion, touch art, for, like art, they have non-linear communication with their audience, an instant recognition of a situation."[1]

In other words, they were like Don's pitch.

The recognition *was* instant: Polaroid sold millions of cameras for the first time in 1961.

1. Robert Glatzer, *The New Advertising: The Great Campaigns from Avis to Volkswagen* (New York: Citadel Press, 1971), 34.

# McCANN-ERICKSON: A LOOSE ALLIANCE OF WARRING CHIEFS

Don Draper's revulsion at being sold off to McCann-Erickson has to do both with his free-pony-roaming the-silvery-plains sense of individualism and also McCann-Erickson's noxious reputation in the 1960s. "Giantism" was their business model. Beginning in the early 1960s, McCann-Erickson, then known as Interpublic Group, gobbled up midsize shops and retained them under one umbrella, but still forced them to compete for clients. This had an upside: two agencies could be under the Interpublic parent company with one shop servicing American Airlines and the other shop servicing TWA. And a downside: the fear, at the time, was there would be leaks and betrayals between agencies. In 1964, Nestlé left McCann-Erickson because the agency also serviced Carnation. Continental also withdrew its business because Interpublic was in bed with other airlines. "Bigness is an evil," a Nestlé executive explained, "that strains relationships which ten years ago were very warm and close."[1] Even the copywriting dynamo Draper Daniels felt the chill for the brief period he worked at McCann. He wrote in his autobiography of McCann:

"It seemed to me that my new comrades in arms greeted me with a friendliness that was somewhat less than underwhelming. Every time I walked down the halls for the first few weeks, I felt as if invisible knives were whistling past my ears. Young & Rubicam had been a disciplined army. McCann-Erickson was a loose alliance of warring chiefs."[2]

The head of McCann, a man named Marion Harper, responded

---

1. Stephen R. Fox, *The Mirror Makers: A History of American Advertising and Its Creators* (Urbana, Ill.: University of Illinois Press, 1997), 266.

2. Draper Daniels, *Giants, Pigmies, and Other Advertising People* (Chicago: Crain Communications, 1974), 104.

publicly about hemorrhaging clients and money one year with this pissy little quote: "We can't support people with little thoughts or little dreams."[3]

Eventually, to keep their clients happy, Harper was sacked. One member of the board of directors for Interpublic said of Marion Harper: "We see him as a genius with one glaring weakness: little sense of people."[4] If you skip forward three years, McCann-Erickson will reclaim its glory with this very un-Draper ad: "I'd like to teach the world to sing" for Coca-Cola.

---

3. Fox, *The Mirror Makers*, 266.

4. Ibid., 267.

# THE TYPOGRAPHY OF TRAVEL:
# AMERICAN AIRLINES[1] BY MEGAN LUBASZKA

Leisurely train travel of the 1950s was outdated and shabby. The jet age of the 1960s and its postwar power class of travelers were eagerly courted by airlines and ad agencies. A hip, forward-thinking company needed to align itself with the flashy new minimalism en vogue if it was going to impress its ideal customer: the modern businessman who valued his time.

It is fitting that American Airlines changed its logo in 1961 to a Helvetica font. Helvetica is neutral. Helvetica is explicitly clear. Helvetica has no formal meaning, no historic roots in carnival posters, newspaper presses, or the Palmer cursive most children were learning. It was newer than the airplanes themselves.

The sans-serif typeface was created in Switzerland and named Neue Haas Grotesk. Marketing the font internationally in 1961, Stempel and Linotype, its parent company, searched for a name that would convey the font's quality and origins. They thought of calling it Helvetia, the Latin name for Switzerland. But the designers didn't want a font named after their homeland, just a name that could convey the cool efficiency and high craftsmanship of their country. So they settled on Helvetica, which simply means "Swiss."

Just like that, according to Mia Fineman of *Slate,* "From the 1960s onward, Helvetica became the font of choice for corporations that wanted to convey an image of modern efficiency with a human face."[2]

More than this, Helvetica fulfilled an emerging need that

---

1. Entry by Megan Lubaszka, writer and infrequent flyer.

2. All quotes from Mia Fineman, "The Helvetica Hegemony: How an Unassuming Font Took Over the World," *Slate*, May 25, 2007.

corporations were unaware they even had: how to achieve consistent, scalable branding. The law of diminishing returns is one that applies to font sizes. Sometimes bigger or smaller is not better, but simply muddled and unreadable.

"Because Helvetica is legible at any scale, companies like Lufthansa and American Airlines adopted the typeface for everything from graphics on the sides of airplanes to cocktail napkins and in-house stationery."

Helvetica was one more thing—timeless. American Airlines has not changed its logo since.

# COOPER STUDIOS:
# MADISON AVE. ARTISANS

Charles E. Cooper was a cigar-chomping, bow-tie-wearing art studio boss who ran a revered art studio during the 1950s and '60s. Unlike Sterling Cooper, which has its own in-house art department, Cooper Studios was a stand-alone illustrators' shop. Cooper, who had refined taste in modern art, employed a breed of illustrators—artisans really—that Sal lamented was being wiped out by photography.

Cooper Studios illustrator Murray Tinkelman explained to a trade magazine (*Illustration*) why he quit his job in the late 1950s to go work for Cooper. "I was working staff at Wallace Brown Greeting Cards and my wife was pregnant. I was home and I was so, like, clinically depressed by the mechanical and the color separations and the hideous work I was doing at Wallace Brown. I literally could not show up at work. So I called in sick." Tinkelman was at home flipping through 1956's Art Director's Annual to pass the day and came across a page that changed his career.

"I came across a stopper—an absolutely beautiful pencil drawing of some people leaning up against a wire mesh fence looking in at a baseball batting situation. It was a marvelous drawing—beautifully composed, beautifully drawn with a modern flair to it."[1]

Tinkelman picked up the phone and scheduled a job interview for the next day. After scrutinizing his portfolio for more than an hour, Cooper brought Tinkelman on for ninety bucks a week. He became part of a shop that revolutionized old illustration concepts through the use of perspective, dimension, and color in its drawings.

Tinkelman was a contemporary of midcentury superstar illustrator Bernie Fuchs. "It was gorgeous," Tinkelman remarked when he first came across Fuchs's work at Cooper Studios. Tinkelman

---

1. Neil Shapiro, "Illustrating an Era: The Charles E. Cooper Studio," *Illustration* 18 (Winter 2007): 53.

called over to two other well-respected Cooper illustrators to take a look, Joe Bowler and Coby Whitmore. Whitmore was speechless. Bowler said, "I don't know who the hell did this, but the business is never going to be the same."[2]

It never was.

For close to fifteen years, Cooper Studios supplied the publishing and advertising industries with top-grade illustrations. But the market shifted too rapidly for the studio to compete; Cooper Studios eventually lost its foothold when the demand for photography supplanted exquisite drawing.

---

2. Ibid., 57.

# AN ILLUSTRATOR'S ICON:
# BERNIE FUCHS[1] BY DAVE WILKIE

Whether he was illustrating a golf course, a car, a dinner party, or a yachting excursion, Bernie Fuchs could tell a story. His images draw you in, and you find yourself assigning roles to the many players in one of his illustrations, much like you do at the airport when sitting around waiting, watching strangers and wondering where they come from and what they're doing.

This ad has no copy, and Fuchs could've sold it to any number of whiskey makers or even a tuxedo emporium.

Oh yes, we're going to Mardi Gras, but we will do New Orleans in style. We've got a balcony right above the main parade route, and a private room reserved at the club.

Everyone is in a tux, everyone is clearly buzzed. Notice that across the street some lesser men of more modest means also stand on balconies, but they wear neckties and plain suits or sports coats. Fuchs plays to the elitist in us, wanting us to taste the good life, or to quote Steve Martin in *The Jerk*, "*Be* somebody!"

These gents are older, graying or gray, and that golden spirit they swirl in their tumblers is the nectar of success, the drink that is the reward, if not the very reason for their great accomplishments. The man in the back has reached such lofty heights in the firm that he is able to sport that most telling accessory—a mustache!

The men on the balconies across the street do not hold drinks, and if they don't start drinking whatever it is these men drink, they will always stand a balcony lower.

Failures.

---

1. Entry by Dave Wilkie. He is an ad man who appreciates illustrations and blogs at *Where's My Jetpack*.

When you're flipping through a magazine, wherever magazines are flipped through these days, few ads will stop you and take you in. Fuchs needed few words, and copywriters probably liked working with him because he made their job easy, maybe needing a simple headline or tagline to complete—if not ruin—the ad.

# THE MINIMAL REALISM OF MORTON SALT: **CHARLEY HARPER**

There are framed Morton Salt ads in most everyone's office at Sterling Cooper.[1] Minimalist master Charley Harper is their illustrator. Harper drew for Procter & Gamble, Ivory, Morton Salt, and *Ford Times* magazine throughout the 1950s and early 1960s.

When asked to describe his unique visual style, Harper responded: "When I look at a wildlife or nature subject, I don't see the feathers in the wings, I just count the wings. I see exciting shapes, color combinations, patterns, textures, fascinating behavior and endless possibilities for making interesting pictures. I regard the picture as an ecosystem in which all the elements are interrelated, interdependent, perfectly balanced, without trimming or unutilized parts; and herein lies the lure of painting; in a world of chaos, the picture is one small rectangle in which the artist can create an ordered universe."[2]

Harper took hard-edged two-dimensional shapes and reduced them to colorful lines and curves. His idea was to "push simplification as far as possible without losing identification."[3] His "minimal realism," as he called it, had the fundamental elements of modern midcentury style: sleek lines, vibrant colors, simple form.

1. The Morton Umbrella Girl logo was not created by Harper—she first appeared on its packaging in 1914. In 1911, Morton's first advertising campaign for a series of ads in *Good Housekeeping* created the idea for the girl and her slogan, "When it rains it pours," meaning it wouldn't clump, even in damp weather. The 1956 redesign was drawn by illustrator Lucia Lerner.

2. Rick Lewis, "Wildlife Artist Charley Harper Dead at 84," *People, Land and Water*, June 12, 2007.

3. Todd Oldham, *Charley Harper: An Illustrated Life* (Los Angeles: AMMO Books, 2009), 2.

# BETHLEHEM STEEL: A LOVE LETTER TO INFRASTRUCTURE[1] BY MEGAN LUBASZKA

Forging, casting, welding, smithing, blasting, heating, hammering, fabricating: the story of America is the story of steel. This great expanse of country, with its vague, infinite landscape, was wrestled into submission with a series of grids and perimeters. Crisscrossing interstates to connect one place to everyplace. Rivers straitjacketed in concrete to make electricity and provide drinking water. Downtowns that scraped the sky.

Yet, Bethlehem Steel ads from the 1960s hawk canned soft drinks and patio furniture. It's a shame they didn't go with Sterling Cooper after all. Sal's bold perspective of the Brooklyn Bridge and the city's shoulders looming beyond capture an essential truth: without steel, there would be no New York City. There would be no America.

The executives from Bethlehem Steel are unimpressed and confused—it looks like a WPA ad. The iconic posters of the Depression era share the themes of progress and stability as well as a simple graphic style.

Sal's drawing is a shadowy sketch, minimal and absolute, as monoliths rise from a tiny island that would become the center of the world. The city is reduced to the engineer's aesthetic. It is presented without detail and frill, pure Platonic volumes distilled to their essence: rebar and piles and beams and columns.

Sure, the light, cheap, cold-rolled sheets of steel and all their possible uses as commodities in the suburban home were innovative. Yet this was the time of audacious infrastructure projects by national, state, and local governments. Why ignore the steel mills, smokestacks, cement pits and piles, the quarries, the reservoirs, the basins, flood channels, huge canyon dams, freeways, washes, rail yards, airports, and military bases?

---

1. Entry by Megan Lubaszka, writer and lapsed architect.

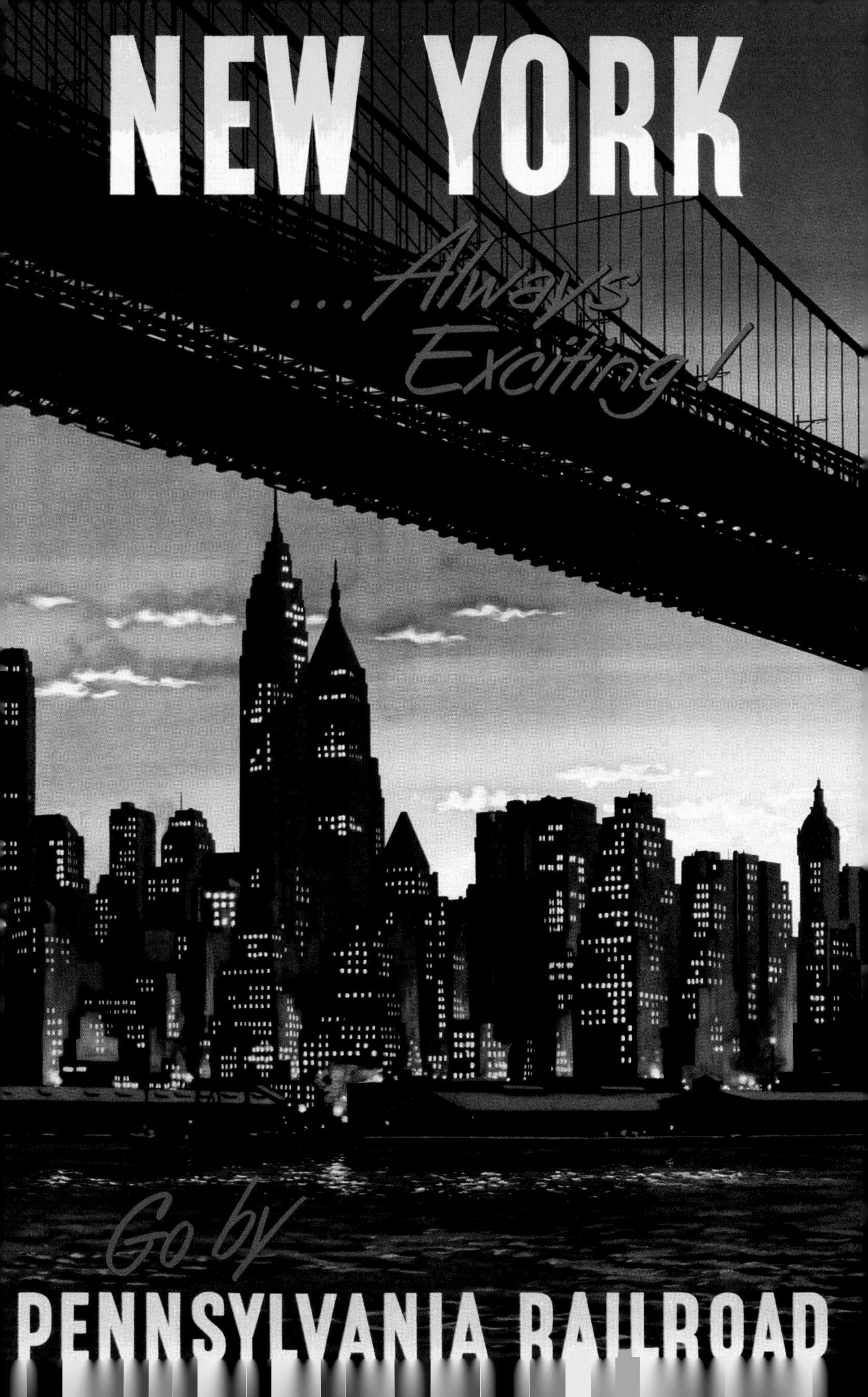
NEW YORK
...Always Exciting!
Go by
PENNSYLVANIA RAILROAD

# Ceil Chapman's dreams begin with a
## *maidenform* girdle

**the dream of a dress.**

Ceil Chapman's black and brief beauty of whisper-soft silk crepe. The chic of the sultry sleeves which barely exist, the V (for vamp?) neckline, and a whittled, belittled waist from which the tempo draws its artistry. Clearly, the whole manner of Ceil Chapman dictates that the figure of fall fashion is slim, slimmer, slimmest (helped to who knows what extent by the girdle beneath)?

**the dream of a girdle:**

Maidenform's Variation* girdles are weightless with all the wings that are the very soul of restraint and self-control. Seamless (and seemingly endless) powers of persuasion gently prompt your figure to sheath-worthy trimness. Select from seven flattering, figuring Variation styles. In winter white that stays white. Pantie girdle illustrated just 2.95. Other Variations* (all machine washable) up to 5.00.

# MAIDENFORM: TIE ME UP/TIE ME DOWN

What kind of woman would be compelled to blow money based solely on the utility of a garment? Up until the mid-1950s bras were marketed for their functionality. It wasn't until the postwar era that undergarments were mass-produced and sold as objects of seduction and allure.

"Bras are for men," Paul Kinsey explains to the creative crew regarding their Playtex account. "Women want to see themselves the way *men* see them." For Paul, and his oft-bemoaned male gaze, there were only two ways for women to be seen: Jackie or Marilyn.

Chaste or easy; Betty or Joan (pity for Peggy—the boys inform her that she's more of the sexless, Irene Dunne type). The Madonna/Whore dichotomy that Paul bases the Playtex campaign on has, of course, been one of the great sexual hang-ups of men and women since they've had clothes to slip off of each other.

Even a man as emotionally complicated as Don Draper—and what great man isn't?—succumbs to the ancient binary. In the same episode that Don yanks Bobbie Barrett's bob, ties her to the bed, and tells her to stop talking, he also chastises Betty for going to the public pool in a bikini because it makes her look desperate. But leave it to Don, with his fits of forced introspection, to recognize the woeful contradictions of manhood: after a shower, with a towel slung around his waist, Don is having a shave when Sally plops herself down by him and announces "I'm not gonna talk—I don't want you to cut yourself."

Don abruptly dismisses his daughter and gives the mirror a requisite thousand-yard stare, well aware, presumably, that his daughter will one day get tied up and summarily told to shut up or commanded to dress down and be modest by some other man.

# 2

**STYLE**

Models in Christian Dior.

# A FASHION REVELATION: THE NEW LOOK

Swathed around Joan's sumptuous hips or bubbling over Betty's delicate shoulders is a clothing style called the New Look. In 1947 Christian Dior introduced this line of women's clothing, which revolutionized women's fashion and its manufacture.

Up until Dior's models sauntered down the runway, the fashion world had been suffering the deprivations of World War II. In response to women working on factory floors, war rations, and the morose atmosphere that comes with something like economic devastation from warring empires, clothes coming out of Europe were plain and functional. Dior's 1947 line rejuvenated the fashion world with his voluptuous new collection, which used yards and yards of luxurious fabrics to infuse clothes with femininity. The line combined long billowing skirts with folded pleats and narrow waistlines; soft, rounded sleeves; flowing dresses; hourglass silhouettes; and accessories such as umbrellas and gloves. "It's quite a revelation, dear Christian," Carmel Snow, the editor of *Harper's Bazaar*, remarked at the time. "Your dresses have such a new look."

French couture patrons (i.e., rich ladies) were in a frenzy to wrap themselves in such elegant and cutting-edge designs. But Dior's biggest clients were Americans: Hollywood stars, New York socialites, and—most important—department store buyers, who purchased

Christian Dior dress.

exclusive rights to individual designs to be reproduced by their factory houses. Even discount retailers were allowed to attend Dior's private fashion shows if they promised to buy the rights to nine outfits. Clothing companies would send sketch artists to European fashion shows, copy the design, and mass-produce inexpensive clothing for the American population.

The mega-industrialization created by the war allowed American and European manufacturers to meticulously reproduce Dior's designs cheaply and en masse. This manufacturing miracle created what we now refer to today as ready-to-wear fashion and voilà! Secretaries, shop girls, and middle-class housewives started looking svelte.

The New Look crested in the mid-1950s and began to roll back around 1960–61. You can see the evolution when you compare the hemlines and fitted styles of the women's skirts and sweaters on *Mad Men*.

In 1962 Betty, Peggy, and most of the steno pool's style is grounded in the New Look. The ladies' skirts are flowing, nipped at the waist, and come down past their knees. The blouses of the phone operators (and particularly Peggy) are boxy around the bust. Joan's style is more emblematic of an emergent fashion trend generated by Coco Chanel's design house: pencil skirts worn closer to the hip, wrapped snugly around the back and thigh and tapered down right at the knees, along with tighter cardigan sweaters with smaller lapels.

# "PUT YOUR HAIR IN CURLERS":
## AT THE HOME SALON

After a tearful day on the job, Don tells Peggy to "Go home, put your curlers in."

Sage advice. Curlers and hair spray were two innovations of the late 1950s that revolutionized hairstyling. The mass manufacture of these products changed what was once considered a salon splurge to be an at-home, accessible treat for women. World War II had

been hard for so many: the corn-fed GIs in crumbling Europe, the residents of Nagasaki, the frostbitten soldiers on the Russian front, and of course, the beleaguered working women whose femininity was sacrificed for wartime scrimping and labor! So when the boys came home, the curlers came out and hair got big. This is why Kurt, Sterling Cooper's freelance artist, refers to Peggy's no-frills, pulled-back ponytail as "old style" and said it was preventing her from finding the right man (true, Peggy's utilitarian 'do belongs in a dacha rather than a midcentury Manhattan office).

The emerging styles were lavish bouffants, flipped tips, and French twists. They began sprouting up during the late 1950s and reached fad proportions when Jackie Kennedy began her tenure as first lady in 1961. *Life* magazine described Jackie's hair as elegantly European and "aristocratic" in its delicacy.

A lady of Peggy's age would have been subject to the nightly ritual of looping her locks around plastic curlers, wrapping a scarf around her crown, and awakening to swooping flips and curls. To keep the coiffed swirls in place, ladies embraced hair spray. By 1964 hair spray dethroned lipstick as the nation's number-one beauty aid.

This style, was of course, rather labor-intensive. So whereas Joan or Betty could take the time to twirl and tease her hair up into a sumptuous puff, a working mom/divorcée like Helen Bishop wore hers down and straight, presumably because she did not have the time be so meticulously styled as the other ladies.

# *LA DOLCE* DRAPER:
# BETTY'S EUROPEAN MAKEOVER

During the few hours that Betty and Don spend out of their Roman hotel room, Betty gets a radical Euro makeover. A prim Ossiningite (with coiffed curls and cardigans) morphs into a lacquered sex bomb.

Betty slinks onto a Via Strada café patio in a mini cocktail dress with a plunging neckline, an elaborate updo, outsize lashes, oversize pearls, and the requisite European pout.

So who was the prototype for Betty's baroque makeover? One possibility is Brigitte Bardot during her Euro sex kitten period. In a 1961 profile of the then twenty-six-year-old actress, *Life* magazine tried to pinpoint what made Bardot's on-screen and offscreen persona so appealing to both mass audiences and the European intelligentsia:

> Roger Vadim, Brigitte's first husband, close friend, and often her director, thinks he knows. Vadim says, "Women are passing through a terrible crisis. Brigitte symbolizes their strivings for equality in conduct with men. That is why her real fans are not men, as some think, but women." Novelist Marguerite Duras, who wrote *Hiroshima Mon Amour,* says the opposite: "Bardot represents the unexpressed desires of males for infidelity," she argues. "Many women do not like Brigitte. They never look her in the face. They look sideways, shrinking away. They see in her disaster."[1]

The other major influence was very likely Anita Ekberg, a bronzed blonde with a loose style that oozed sexuality. In *La Dolce*

1. "France's Far-Out Sex Siren," *Life* 51, no. 4 (July 28, 1961): 85.

*Vita,* Fellini's masterpiece, she played a Swedish-American movie star (Sylvia) who sweeps into Rome and entrances several men, including the achingly handsome Marcello Mastroianni. In "The Souvenir" episode of Season Three, Betty sits by a fountain and flirts coolly with the men around her while Don looks on.

The image of Betty before the geysers, toying with strong-jawed men, immediately calls to mind the scene in *La Dolce Vita* that immortalized Ekberg: a rapturous blonde in a full-length gown, elegantly sloshing through the Fontana di Trevi just because she could.

# THE MEN IN GRAY FLANNEL SUITS

The gray flannel suit gets a bad rap; the single-breasted three-buttoned narrow-lapel jacket and tapered trouser is cultural short-hand for the stultifying conformity of the 1950s and early '60s (with the accompanying necktie serving as a metaphorical noose). No other dress style of the modern era elicits such scorn as the gray flannel suit. This is thanks, in part, to the 1960 book *The Man in the Gray Flannel Suit* and the Gregory Peck movie based on the same title. The suit in Sloan Wilson's story is emblematic of a pervasive soullessness in the mechanized world, making men numb to themselves, their families, and their morals.

"If we regard any sort of standardized dress as uniform, then it is easy to treat the man in the gray flannel suit as equivalent to the National Guardsman," Joseph Heath and Andrew Potter wrote in their stellar book, *Nation of Rebels*, of the suit's reputation. "The natural alliance with the capitalism of the military-industrial complex is thus revealed through the fact that everyone involved is wearing a uniform of some sort. Here come the cops, here come the suits, here comes The Man." But the reason for the mass adoption of the suit was not, as Heath and Potter point out, due to thoughtless conformity, but rather that men didn't really own very many clothes before the late 1960s. As men moved off the factory floor and into a corporate building, the new standardized uniform became the gray flannel suit. From lowly office drone to FBI spook or GM executive, the men riding the train into Grand Central wore the same thing (sometimes accented with a brimmed hat, tweed overcoat, or a handy umbrella).

The gray suit was an acceptable daily wardrobe: it didn't require much upkeep, nor did it vary from season to season. And while yes, the suit was a type of uniform, imposing the historical verdict that

Gregory Peck in
*The Man in the Gray Flannel Suit.*

men who donned the outfit did so out of unquestioned conformity is too simplistic.

According to a 1964 *Time* magazine article, "The Masculine Mode," the American male over thirty actually preferred to dress similarly to everyone around him. "If one of his colleagues—or two of them—turns up in the same outfit he is wearing, he does not feel embarrassed, as would his wife. He feels reassured."

There is a sense of comfort and belonging created by uniforms. In Don's case, as for most men in gray flannel suits, their business uniform allowed them to signal a sense of privilege and status that a farm boy transplanted onto Madison Avenue would not generally be able to access. Indeed, it's unlikely that Don would ever think he was less free than the protohippies holed up in Midge's loft. Don confidently strides out the door, high on weed he'd been smoking with Midge and her buddies, and tips his brimmed hat to the cops busting Midge's neighbors next door. It's Don's suit that allows him to move fluidly through and above Fourteenth Street.

# "IT MATTERS TO ME THAT YOU'RE IMPRESSED": PETE'S PREP SCHOOL STYLE

Pete Campbell is prep school to his core. From his neatly embroidered white tennis shorts to his tidy side part to his petulant sense of entitlement, Pete is also the best dressed of the ad men in terms of fit and polish. So where does he get it? A personal tailor? Brooks Brothers? Boutiques on Nantucket? While Pete does have the traditional Ivy League look, which was almost uniformly outfitted by Brooks Brothers, his sartorial sense trends a bit younger—men of Pete's age and ilk dressed in J. Press.[1]

Christian Chensvold, fashion writer, founder and editor of *Ivy Style*, interviewed Denis Black, the manager of the Cambridge J. Press store, about the store's historic influence on young men of means:

cc: At what point, and how, did the J. Press go from being collegiate—it was a youth-oriented brand for many decades. . . .
DB: When you say "collegiate" you're thinking in terms of today. This business was started in 1902, and from then until around 1967, everyone on a college campus wore a jacket and tie. It was a young gentleman's look. The Press family began by going door-to-door at dormitories at Yale,

---

1. In an interview about *Mad Men, Ivy Style* founder Christian Chensvold described why men who had never set foot on an Ivy League campus would be compelled to adopt the style: "Sometime in the 1950s, men who worked in Madison Avenue advertising agencies wholeheartedly embraced the Ivy League look. While it was partly no doubt due to workers who'd graduated from Eastern colleges, where they'd picked up the taste for natural-shouldered suits, button-down collars, and rep and club ties, two other factors probably figure into it as well. First off, the advertising industry doesn't have the most wholesome image, and the Ivy League look would have conferred upon ad men redeeming signifiers to their varied clients: It was both modern (showing they were in tune with the times) and yet discreetly respectable. Next is the question of geography. During the time that *Mad Men* is set, the epicenter of the Ivy League look was Forty-fourth and Madison, where Brooks Brothers, J. Press, Chipp, and Paul Stuart were all located. This is just a few blocks from Grand Central Terminal, making this cluster of classic American menswear shops convenient for men like Don Draper, commuting each day through Grand Central on Metro North.

and then traveling to all the prep schools by train. So when you say "collegiate" or "youthful" dressing, there was no such thing in those days.

Throughout the first three seasons of *Mad Men* Pete has sported the requisite prep style wear: toggle coat; cable knit pullover; narrow lapels; easy lines; and, most important, suit jackets without padding. (Eventually, this would be called the natural shoulder look.) The prep look is unabashedly upper-class, meant to look expensive—but never gaudy—and effortless at the same time. Even

Pete's hair is prep-influenced. It's cropped closer than Don's in an effort to maintain the clean-cut look. Rather than visualizing a style icon like Cary Grant in a gray flannel suit, think more along the lines of popular TV host Dick Clark, the friendly, unthreatening ambassador to America's youth.

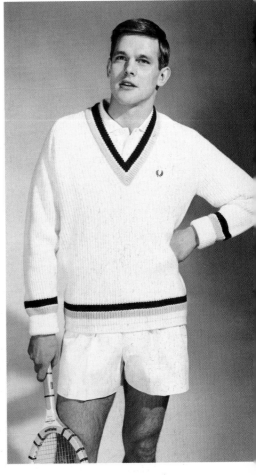

However, there are some trendy, nontraditional twists Pete incorporates into his look. His most radical choice? The skinny tie. "There is clearly some Rat Pack influence," Chensvold told me in an interview on *Mad Men*'s menswear.

"Pete really is a prep school kid, so that's no affectation. Also, precisely because of that reason I believe that that kind of guy would be above anything trendy, having nothing but contempt for it. From my interviews, guys at that time were really closed-minded, and Pete is a WASP. Anything trendy would've been for Jews and Catholics. There would be Brooks Brothers/J. Press and nothing else."

Prep-inspired sartorial choices began to stretch outside of the elite campuses around 1967. With the tremendous cultural shift in fashion, politics, and sex, dressing like a prep meant you flaunted your conservative sensibilities: even if you didn't go to Princeton you could still set yourself apart from greasers or the SoHo-bohos.

# A STREAMLINED MAN: **THE SKINNY TIE**

While women like Betty wore dresses that flowed out from their waistlines and bubbled out over their shoulders, men's dress style contracted in the early '60s. Collars were smaller, lapels narrowed, silhouettes shrank, belts thinned, and ties got skinny. The postwar man was streamlined. Denis Black, a manager for the men's clothing store J. Press, believes that the demand for a smaller suit came from postwar exhaustion.

"When guys came back from World War II they were shattered. Their only thought was to get into college and get a career started. Their lives had been complicated enough by the war. And that simple, stable look. . . . I mean, for years we lived off IBM and the FBI [employees], because that was the look. It's the simplicity of it all."[1]

Black is right, of course. The compression in dress had to do with the postwar desire for simplicity, but it was also inspired by a modernist aesthetic that held steady influence over architecture, textiles, transportation, and fashion beginning from the interwar years and ebbing by the late 1960s.[2]

Tear-shaped trains, Frank Lloyd Wright's horizontal facades, seamless chairs: all parts flow together in one unbroken rhythm. Men's suits followed step: suit pants were trimmer in the legs and flat in front (pleats were a thing of the past). Blazers lost one of their three buttons and tended to be made from synthetics. The broad, boxy look of men's suits was replaced by sleek, uninterrupted

1. Christian Chensvold, "Tradition and Change: The J. Press Interview," *Ivy Style*, July 13, 2009.

2. In 1931, Russel Wright captured the modernist aesthetic in everyday life with this gripe: "Why can't someone, a Museum of Modern Art or a New York World's Fair, put on a exhibition in which they dramatize all design that is American? First, let them parade those envious developments free from any inferiority complexes. Our bridges. Our roads. Our factory machinery, our sky scrapers . . . roll out our trick cocktail gadgets, our streamlined ice boxes, our streamlined pencil sharpeners. Let them show our electric light bulbs on white velvet like jewels. The work of Frank Lloyd Wright. Our gasoline stations. Our movie theaters. Our cafeterias . . . our handsome business machines . . . our gleaming fat automobiles." (*Design 1935–1965: What Modern Was* [New York: Abrams, 2001], 75)

lines. Streamline in fashion allowed efficiency without sacrificing elegance.

The skinny tie of the 1960s is what gave modern menswear an almost lyrical beauty (when done correctly). The tie traced along the button line and injected a sense of color without disrupting the surface of the suit. When essayist David Rakoff traveled to Paris to see couture up close, the graceful, straight lines of a Dior dinner jacket were described as "the goddess Siva lowering a window shade."[3]

The skinny tie would be the pull string.

3. David Rakoff, *Don't Get Too Comfortable* (New York: Anchor Books, 2005), 147.

Attendee of a Yale/Harvard alumni
jazz party in 1977, New York.

## THE PSEUDOREBELLION OF
## PAUL KINSEY: A MAN AND HIS BEARD

Paul Kinsey swills his rum in a fancy tumbler during his rock 'n'
roll housewarming party while his guests sip from jars. When Joan
asks why he gets the fancy glass, Paul says, "There's a ship that
went down in 1871, and the casks of rum were on it—it was a very
good year. And it sank, and they washed up on shore two years ago,
and they sold 180 bottles, and *I* have one."

"But not a sofa," Joan replies.

Poor Paul! He just wants to be different. Can't you tell: A
Princeton grad with his gaudy pipe, silk scarf, dodgy neighborhood

apartment, and, most important, a woolly beard. Paul is the only man at Sterling Cooper with facial hair—an overt at sneer at Eisenhower conformity. And while he moons about politics and authenticity, Paul is ultimately a firm enforcer of the status quo.

But Joan Holloway, with her earthy sensibilities, can smell a phony. Paul is terrified to break into Bert Cooper's office to sneak a peek at a Rothko painting, and rats out his compatriots to her when they do. Without pause he brushes off plans to join his girlfriend and the Freedom Riders to register voters in the violent South to go, instead, to an aerospace conference in Los Angeles. When the British occupation of Sterling Cooper begins, Paul whines to his coworkers that he likes "this company the way it is."

Paul is a conservative man when it comes to ads: he clings to the prerevolutionary style of virtuous copy. Sure, his prose is fancy, but it never elicits the emotional reaction that was emblematic of the new style in advertising (which Don and Peggy so thoroughly embrace). In his pitch to Don on Mohawk Airlines, Pampers, and Gillette, Paul touts the merits of the product instead of creating some kind of narrative about the person who buys the product. Paul's finest moment was when he came up with the simple slogan for Playtex ("Jackie or Marilyn?"). But he is too enamored of his own uniqueness to actually make any substantial change within Sterling Cooper. Make no mistake; Paul is no rebel. He just likes to dress as one.

# 3

# WORKING GIRLS

Harry N. Hirschberg, head of Hecht's department store, in 1958.

# RACHEL MENKEN **AT THE BARGAIN BIN**

Department store heiress Rachel Menken and her retail dynasty are in a branding crisis. The team of gentile ad men hired to elevate the status of her Fifth Avenue store have instead offered her coupons, bargain bins, and a basement sale: the essential qualities of those "Jewish department stores." Those stores featured slogans such as:

> We Keep Busy Being Brooklyn's Store (Abraham & Straus)
> Nobody But Nobody Undersells Gimbels
> The Thrifty Store for Thrifty People (Snellenburg's)

The nerve of some goys.

Rachel and her specialty store closely resemble Bay Ridge–based Kleinfeld. Built in 1941, Kleinfeld became the epicenter for discount bridal wear in the borough. A father/daughter team of Viennese immigrants named Jack and Hedda (Chosen People, naturally) ran the store.

Hedda, eventual owner of Kleinfeld, said this about their Brooklyn bridal nook: "People would say, 'Why did you stay in Bay Ridge? It is because we had the best working staff. It was a classy labor market. The seamstresses and the salespeople had very high standards but didn't like the idea of traveling to the city every day, so they came here and they had an outlet for their talents, and it was very good for the reputation of the store."

But then in 2005 Kleinfeld abandoned Brooklyn for the city. Hedda's description of the store could have come right out of Menken's (incredulous) pitch to Don: "The new Kleinfeld location will be dramatically more spacious and elegant, but one thing that will not change is our focus on our customer, which is the magic behind Kleinfeld."

"Say it ain't so," the *Brooklyn Paper* lamented, "first the Dodgers and now Kleinfeld."[1]

---

1. All quotes from "Kleinfeld Quits Bay Ridge," *Brooklyn Paper*. May 28, 2005.

# HOW TO BE A BETTY: MODELING IN THE 1950S

Given her modeling background, it's no wonder Betty is big on appearances. Before modeling was awash with coke-addled tanorexic teenagers, it was an industry for "nice girls," plucky, pretty young ladies who wanted to swish around department stores, a local 4-H club, and even a small runway show for the newest manufactured styles. If you were lucky enough to be immortalized in an advertisement, there were some serious forms of etiquette to uphold. A model was expected to be well-mannered, well-groomed, and entirely made-up before a photo shoot. From a 1958 modeling pamphlet on what to include in your model bag:

- Half slip
- Strapless bra
- Dress shields
- Extra hose (seamless)
- Black opera pumps
- Clean, short white gloves (fabric and string)
- Strand of pearls
- Pearl choker
- Two pairs of earrings (pearls and simple gold)
- Clean comb, spray net
- Scarf to protect hair

Further, the pamphlet echoes Betty's philosophy about self-image:

Beautiful models and beautiful diamonds are not unlike. Both evolve by perfecting each and every facet so that the

Models on the streets of Philadelphia showing off fur swimsuits, circa 1960.

whole product or being will shine with brilliance. By giving all the phases of modeling the attention they deserve, you'll polish every facet of the diamond—and the diamond is, of course, you![1]

So, it's not terribly surprising that Betty shows up to her big Coca-Cola shoot in an evening gown and pearls. What Betty missed, though, in the few years since she gave up modeling for motherhood was that the elegant woman—posed motionless in stately living rooms or whitewashed studios—was supplanted by the 1960s "single girl" aesthetic.

Generally shot outdoors or in motion, models went from being passive to active subjects in photo spreads with blurry economic status: she could be a secretary or a socialite, but regardless, she was simply invigorated by product X! In her essay on fashion photography trends of the midcentury, Hilary Radner described the single-girl mode as "waif-like and adolescent" in both looks and goals. She just longed to "be glamorous and adored by men (in the plural) while economically independent."[2] The single-girl imagery hinted at the coming transformation that would eventually hit Betty's generation—and maybe even Betty herself.

1. "How to Look Like a Model," prepared in cooperation with John Robert Powers School.

2. Hilary Radner, "On the Move: Fashion Photography and the Single Girl in the 1960s," in *Fashion Cultures: Theories, Explorations, and Analysis,* edited by Stella Bruzzi and Pamela Church Gibson (London: Routledge, 2000), 128.

# WHAT THEY DIDN'T TEACH IN SECRETARY SCHOOL

Peggy Olson joins the Sterling Cooper steno pool wide-eyed and fresh out of Miss Deaver's Secretarial School. Joan, the overseer of the squadron of working girls, gives Peggy a job description for her new position that Miss Deaver probably didn't cover. Peggy diligently notes Joan's summation of her job description, probably writing it down in shorthand: "He may act like he wants a secretary, but most of the time they're looking for something between a mother and a waitress. And the rest of the time, well. . . ."

Peggy gets the message: by the end of the day, she's purchased aspirin, rye, and birth control. Also coming out of her first week's salary: chocolate, bath salts, and carnations, some tiny bribes to suck up to the telephone operators with, a small deposit in the bank of office politics.

The prevalence of the XX chromosome in the steno pool is thanks to the Remington typewriter, created in 1873. Before the Remington, the professional secretary, responsible for bookkeeping and correspondence, was dominated by educated lower-class males. In order to ease the typewriter into offices, Remington used women in their advertisements and catalogs operating the new technology. As a result, secretarial work came to be associated with women (consider that the lone male secretary walking the halls of Sterling Cooper was the British toady from Puttnam, Powell and Lowe). Remington and other companies created schools that offered typing instruction. These would eventually become secretarial schools, the most esteemed of which was the Katharine Gibbs School.

Judith Krantz's bestselling novel *Scruples* describes what it was like to be a student at Gibbs in 1963:

Secretarial trainees try out new technology in 1961.

Out of the corner of her eye she was aware that someone was stationed by the elevator door checking out each girl for gloves, hat, dress, and makeup, of which there must not be much. . . . Were they seriously expecting her to be able to take one hundred words a minute in shorthand and type faultlessly at a minimum of sixty words a minute by the time she had completed her course? They were indeed.[1]

At Miss Deaver's, Peggy would have learned how to take and transcribe shorthand, speedy typing, and the act of making carbon copies. Luckily, she had Joan to help her navigate, as *Sex and the Office* author Helen Gurley Brown put it, the "intrigue, romance, coquetry, duels and excitement" of the midcentury Manhattan office.[2]

---

1. Judith Krantz, *Scruples* (New York, Bantam, 1989), 123.

2. Helen Parmalee, "Married Girl," n.d., box 21, folder 6, Helen Gurley Brown Papers, Sophia Smith Collection, Smith College, Northampton, Massachusetts.

# COFFEE, TEA, OR ME?: STEWARDESSES, THE GLAMOUR GIRLS OF THE SKIES

In the third season episode "Out of Town," one of the glamour girls of the air coos over Don as Sal says incredulously, "I've flown a few times, but I've never actually seen a stewardess *that* game."[1]

"Really," Don replies. There is no hint of question in his voice, only a tone of sly, knowing amusement.

In the way casinos still encourage their cocktail waitresses to flirt and seduce in order to glue the clientele to the slot floor, the airlines used to employ a similar service model.

In *The Fifties: A Women's Oral History,* Carla Vincent tells about her time at the McConnell school for stewardesses in Minneapolis: "The emphasis was on charming the passengers. You learned to walk with a book on your head—one book one day, two books the next. We learned makeup and how to do our hair. We all looked pretty much alike, we all had exactly the same makeup and the same haircut."[2]

The pay was paltry, often as little as $225 a month, but the girls gladly traded a sad waitressing job on the ground for the pizzazz of travel and the instant sheen of allure the airline industry offered. It was an easy way for a white woman to barter her country roots for that of a jet-setting cosmopolitan existence and possibly pick up a rich husband in the process.

Stringent recruiters would examine hopeful applicants for dark roots showing evidence of dyeing, the lightest ribbon of a varicose vein, bowed legs, any tendency to gain weight, or a rebellious attitude. A far cry from today's jostled, cramped flying experience

---

1. *Life* magazine celebrated the opening of a new American Airlines facility for training stewardesses in 1958 with the cover story "Glamor Girls of the Air: For Lucky Ones Being Hostess Is the Mostest."

2. Brett Harvey, *The Fifties: A Women's Oral History* (New York: HarperCollins, 1993), 140–41.

of loud babies and nonexistent legroom, the airlines of that time were crafting their own heaven, a paradise in the sky in which a traveler's needs were not merely met but anticipated by a bevy of gorgeous and nearly identical women.

The airlines even drafted legal documents detailing strict beauty requirements. In 1953 American Airlines made a rule of grounding stewardesses on their thirty-second birthday. The official company policy explained why:

> Based on the established qualifications for Stewardesses, which are attractive appearance, pleasant disposition, even temperament, neatness, unmarried status, and the ability and desire to meet and serve passengers. Basic among the qualifications is an attractive appearance. Such an appearance ordinarily is found to a higher degree in young women. Therefore, the establishment of an age limit will best effectuate and preserve the concept of Stewardess service as it is understood in this Company.[3]

Until the gals organized and fought the airlines with unions, stewardesses were simply thought of as fresh, beautiful, and, ultimately, disposable.

---

3. Kathleen M. Barry, *Femininity in Flight: A History of Flight Attendants* (Durham, N.C.: Duke University Press, 2007), 112–13.

# TOUCHING AND FEELING WITH TEACHER: SUZANNE

Sally Draper is acting out after the death of her grandfather. Her grade school teacher, syrupy young idealist Suzanne Farrell, is concerned and wants to talk to the Drapers about Sally's behavior.

A teacher discussing a student's feelings with parents would be flouting classroom management conventions of the early 1960s. It would be considered part of a new and dubious ideology of teaching. Behavioral studies of the 1950s suggested teachers should assume a role of strict authority; if a student was misbehaving, then he or she was expected to be disciplined, not "counseled" the way Sally's teacher (clumsily) attempted to do.

Gilbert Highet's 1960 book *The Art of Teaching* was a definitive guide for young teachers in the classroom. It also provided examples of the changing attitudes of teachers. Highet encourages teachers to shed their roles as petty despots and synthesizers of information and assume a looser, more maternal role, reminding would-be educators that "the young are trying to be energetic and wise and kind. When you remember this, it is impossible not to like them."

The ideology in transition recalled this passage about teaching, from Zoe Heller's book on stuffy old teachers and drippy new do-gooders:

> Many of the younger teachers harbor secret hopes of "making a difference." . . . They, too, want to want conquer their little charges' hearts with poetry and compassion. When I was at teacher training college, there was none of this sort of thing. My fellow students and I never thought of raising self-esteem

or making dreams come true. Our expectations did not go beyond the three *R*s and providing them with some pointers on personal hygiene. Perhaps we were lacking in idealism . . . We might not have fretted much about our children's souls in the old days, but we did send them out into the world knowing how to do long division.[1]

Suzanne softened those cold columns of long division on the chalkboard with some touchy-feelyness.

---

1. Zoe Heller, *What Was She Thinking?* (New York: Picador, 2003), 29.

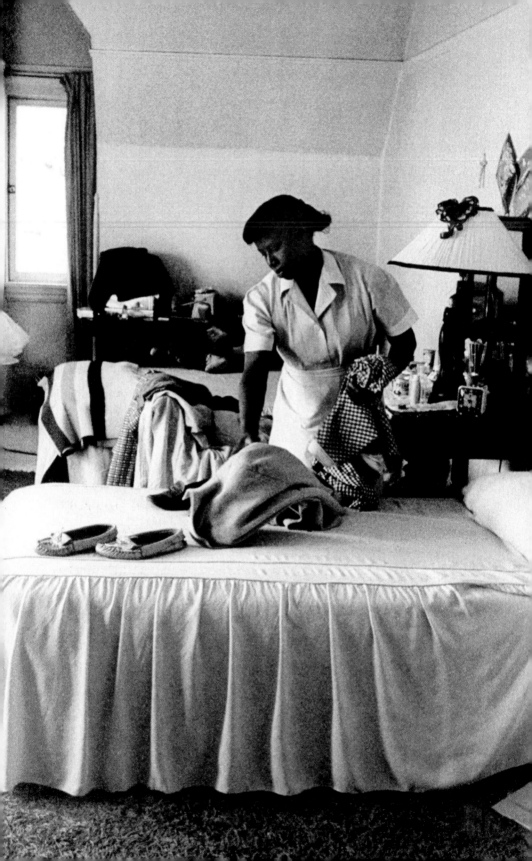

# FIRST SHOTS IN THE NANNY WARS: CARLA

Servants! What an emotionally fraught and ambiguous place they hold in American life. Consider Carla's role in the Draper household. Is she a nanny? Or is she a "cleaning girl"? Is it acceptable to pay another woman to keep the house *and* show a mother's love for her children? Will the children bond to Carla more than they will to their mother? How exactly *were* middle-class suburban housewives supposed to treat the help in 1963?

Well, Betty Draper seems to have none of the answers—nor is she even asking these questions.

"We thought about getting a nanny," Betty tells Roger and his wife on a double dinner date with Don. "We have a girl that comes in, a sort of a housekeeper and sometimes babysitter. I don't let her take the children to play group, but sometimes the park."[1]

With the ranks of the middle class swelling during the postwar era, the dilemma of how to negotiate the possibly explosive territory of household staff responsibilities and family duties—which had been exclusively a problem of the moneyed—plopped into the laps of middle-class suburban mothers. Prior to the economic boom, the lines between domestic employer and employee were made clear and reinforced by the rigid class system and social mores of Victorian society. "Servant culture has a long history in which employer and employee share a code of how they should behave toward one another," Caitlin Flanagan wrote in her essay on the vexing social interactions between moms and nannies.

---

1. Betty grew up wealthy and had a nanny, whom we meet when Betty goes to visit her ailing father. Roger also had a nanny, whom, as his wife vouched, he loved very much. Don scoffs at being raised by a nanny not because he has some opinion on the parental responsibilities of motherhood, but because ordinary folks could not afford nannies before the economic boom of the midcentury. They were a luxury of the rich. It's possible that when Don and Betty "talked about" getting a nanny Don did not want to pay for a full-time or live-in nanny. Betty has no real model for how to treat a part-time maid/babysitter. Betty's muddled expectations of her housekeeper—and Carla's obvious anxiety about overstepping—was likely a common dynamic for this new kind of domestic arrangement.

"Expectations regarding attire, duties, forms of address—all were made manifestly clear."[2]

Nannies and maids were worlds apart. The sole responsibility of nannies was the care of the children—some were formally trained to be maternal surrogates—whereas maids kept the house in order. Flanagan cites Maud Shaw's memoir about serving as nanny to Caroline and John Kennedy Jr., *White House Nannie,* as an example of an ethical way to treat the help. "The seven and a half years I was with her," Shaw wrote reverently about Jackie, "she never asked me to as much as pick up a pin for her. Even in the White House, she never once asked me to do anything that was not strictly within my province."

Betty's expectations of Carla blur all prior boundaries. Though Carla, whom Betty treats as a maid, originally only "came by" in the afternoons, she was also expected to serve as a surrogate mother to Sally and Bobby when Betty was stricken (rightfully) with paranoia and melancholy about Don. Carla is also entrusted with Betty's children for six weeks so that Betty may take a "divorcation" in Reno with Henry Francis.

The nanny-mommy relationship would grow increasingly tense as black women, after centuries of servitude, started leaving domestic work en masse during the late 1960s. Luckily for Betty—and Henry Francis—that was still years away.

---

2. Caitlin Flanagan, "How to Treat the Help?" *Atlantic,* June 2006.

# 4

## SEX

# PEGGY'S PAMPHLET: A GUIDE TO (RESPECTFULLY) GETTING IT ON

Before her new gynecologist enters the room—brandishing a steel speculum in one hand and a lit cigarette in the other—Peggy Olson browses a pamphlet called "It's *Your* Wedding Night."

Sex pamphlets entered doctors' offices around the turn of the century. The Victorian idea was that good girls didn't think about sex until—surprise!—it's your wedding night. In 1900, Ida Craddock published a series of wedding-night etiquette guides. The pamphlet "The Wedding Night" sets out to answer this mystifying question: "What art thou, oh night of mystery and passion? Why shouldst thou be thus enshrouded in an impenetrable veil of secrecy? Are thy joys so pure, so dazzling, so ecstatic, that no outside mortal can look upon thy face and live?" According to Craddock, it's a night to respect the wishes and soothe the fears of your anxious wife. The best way to do this is to avoid "genital contact."

In the majority of cases, no genital union at all should be attempted, or even suggested, upon that night. To the average young girl, virtuously brought up, the experience of sharing her bedroom with a man is sufficient of a shock to her previous maidenly habits, without adding to her nervousness by insisting upon the close intimacies of genital contact. And, incredible as it may sound to the average man, she is usually altogether without the sexual experience which every boy acquires in his dream-life. The average, typical girl does not have erotic dreams. In many cases, too, through the prudishness of parents—a prudishness which is positively criminal—she is not even told beforehand that genital union will be required of her.

But once your bride is ready to receive, other fun tips from the pamphlet include:

- As to the clitoris, this should be simply saluted, at most, in passing, and afterwards ignored as far as possible; for the reason that it is a rudimentary male organ, and an orgasm aroused there evokes a rudimentary male magnetism in the woman, which appears to pervert the act of intercourse, with the result of sensualizing and coarsening the woman. Within the duller tract of the vagina, after a half-hour, or, still better, an hour of tender, gentle, self-restrained coition, the feminine, womanly, maternal sensibilities of the bride will be aroused, and the magnetism exchanged then will be healthful and satisfying to both parties.
- Also, to the bride, I would say: Bear in mind that it is part of your wifely duty to perform pelvic movements during the embrace, riding your husband's organ gently, and, at times, passionately, with various movements, up and down, sideways, and with a semi-rotary movement, resembling the movement of the thread of a screw upon a screw. These

movements will add greatly to your own passion and your own pleasure, but they should not be dwelt in thought for this purpose. They should be performed for the express purpose of conferring pleasure upon your husband, and you should carefully study the results of various movements, gently and tenderly performed, upon him.

✄ "But she might never want it?" My dear sir, you must be indeed lacking in manhood to be unable to arouse sex desire in a bride who loves you with even a halfway sort of affection.[1]

Craddock herself was a bit of a mystic (and eccentric), and conservative reaction to her work led her to commit suicide. But Craddock's emphasis on the sanctity of sex, the fragility of female sexuality, and step-by-step how-tos endured for half a century—even if it lost its wild phrasing.

---

1. Ida Craddock, "The Wedding Night" (n.p., 1900).

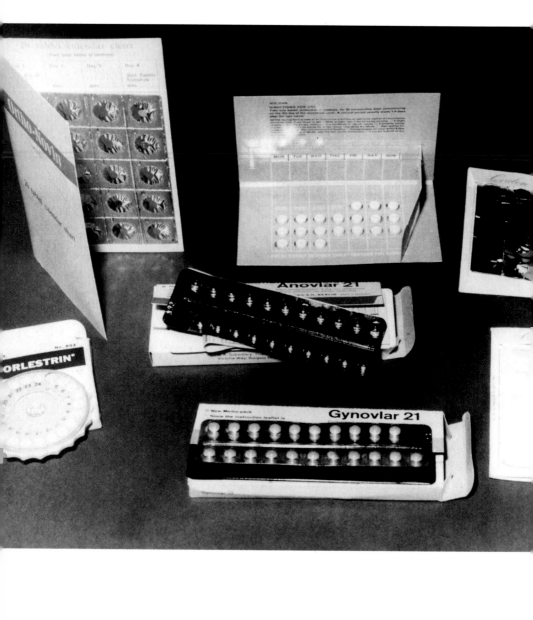

# PREVENTING PEGGY'S OVULATION

After a stern finger-wagging about not becoming the "town pump," Peggy's doctor prescribes her Enovid. Enovid was initially approved by the FDA for therapeutic treatment of menstrual disorders. Two years after it hit the market, more than half a million American women were taking Enovid, presumably for the off-label purpose of fending off pregnancy instead of mediating a nasty case of cramps.

Peggy's doctor threatens to yank away her prescription if she abuses it. Beyond just being an admonishment from a patronizing authority figure, the doctor could take the pill away from Peggy because he was doing her a *favor*. It was not legal in any state in the Union in March 1960 to prescribe a pill for the sole purpose of preventing ovulation.

This is a fact that has been rattled off since *Roe v. Wade* in partisan debates about what women were and were not allowed to do with their wombs, but let's really digest this through the tender body of Peggy Olson. Anytime Peggy wanted to neck with a boy in Bay Ridge or fool around with a rival executive (ahem, Duck Phillips) she would have to be discreet—not only to preserve her reputation and social standing, but also because her doctor could legally take away her contraceptive based on his notions of correct sexual behavior. Peggy's right not to ovulate was based on the judgment of a doctor who referred to her ass as a "fanny."

# YOUNGS FOR RUBBERS

Peggy asks the boy she is necking with in his Brooklyn abode, "Do you have—you know, a Trojan?" This question seems remarkably modern (like 1994 modern) for a twentysomething in the 1960s, but it's absolutely correct: Trojan ran the rubber business in the midcentury and still dominates it today.

Before World War I, condoms were strictly considered instruments of vice. They could really only be purchased in the back of a seedy bar. But once the troops shipped off to fight in Europe to serve in the Great War, condoms became an essential accessory for American boys to fraternize with the locals *as men*.

Sensing the stigma around condoms peeling back after the war, condom patent owner Merle Leland Youngs—a devout Presbyterian from upstate New York—started to advertise his product, Youngs Rubbers, directly to pharmacists and doctors. He put clinically friendly copy in medical catalogues and journals for Youngs Rubbers. In his article on the history of condoms, "The Other Trojan War," Brendan I. Koerner summarized Youngs's marketing strategy: "[Youngs] countered the product's dicey reputation by stressing manufacturing standards and building a state-of-the-art factory in Trenton, N.J., that produced condoms of uniform quality. He also favored austere packaging emblazoned with nothing but a Trojan helmet, a symbol meant to connote protection and virility." Consumers would ask the pharmacists for condoms and take whatever they were handed, and they were most often handed Youngs. But because of the antiquity-themed imagery, it gained the nickname "Trojan." With such a great monopoly on the rubber trade, Youngs would actively sue any other company that tried to impinge on his logo. In 1965 he officially switched the brand name to Trojan.

Today, 70.5 percent of condoms purchased in United States drugstores are Trojan.

A bulletin board of girls at an American base in Germany, 1947.

Helen Gurley Brown at home.

# SEX AND THE SINGLE GIRL

When Don's clingy teacher girlfriend, Suzanne, ambushes him during his morning train commute, she says to him, "I don't care about your marriage or your work or any of that, as long as I know you're with *me*." Don grabs her hand and quietly assures her, though he is clearly terrified by her brazen surprise visit.

Doesn't Suzanne seem a bit too blasé about the whole marriage thing? Maybe not. One of the lady books burning up the best-seller list in 1962 was Helen Gurley Brown's *Sex and the Single Girl*. Brown, through her series of books and thirty-two-year tenure at *Cosmopolitan,* in her own odd way inspired a generation of home wreckers and housewives to lead whatever sexual life made them happy (and rich!). Brown viewed infidelity as an inevitability, so why not chase married men? In a chapter entitled, "The Availables: The Men in Your Life," Brown speaks favorably about affairs with them. "I'm afraid I have a rather cavalier attitude about wives," she wrote.[1] "I think marriage is insurance for the *worst* years of your life. During your best years you don't need a husband. You do need a man of course every step of the way, and they are often cheaper emotionally and a lot more fun by the dozen."

Here's another little gem from the book: "My friend Agnes

---

1. All quotes are from Helen Gurley Brown, *Sex and the Single Girl* (New York: Bernard Geis Associates, 1962).

lives over a garage in one enormous room. . . . A hot plate and ice box make the kitchen, but you can see wonderful old sycamores through the windows." This passage precisely describes Suzanne's apartment. No wonder Brown's message of sexual conquest resonated with her.

Brown's advice wasn't some radical critique on marriage or a purposefully risqué sexual diary. It was dedicated to "mouse-burgers," the girls of poor or modest means who would have no chance of escaping their social caste without a financial boost from a wealthy man. For Brown it was all really about class, because having grown up in an Ozarkian farm encampment, she was around women who didn't have any. Women, aged from labor and child rearing, walked around barefoot and lifted their dresses to pee on the side of the road. Whatever it took to be forever removed from that caste, Brown believed you should take: wife, kids, another mistress, whatever!

"Unlike Madame Bovary, you don't chase the glittering life, you lay a trap for it. You tunnel up from the bottom."

Brown eventually got out of the southern slums herself, went to secretarial school, became a working girl at an ad agency, entered an essay contest for *Glamour,* won, and ended up where all nice girls do: publishing.

## JOAN GOES LIGHTLY **AMONG THE LESBIANS**

It has been said before of Joan, but she does seem to possess some of those uncanny traits of Holly Golightly, the indelible protagonist of Truman Capote's classic *Breakfast at Tiffany's*. Particularly with her choice of roommates.

How could a savvy li'l sex kitten like Joan have not seen her roommate Carol's more-than-a-girl-crush confession coming? Joan just smiled it off and brought men back to their apartment.

Perhaps Joan was doing what Golightly did: Make sure there was no missed opportunity for a lady. Joan, well intentioned but sometimes clumsy, believes that she can teach the girls in her life how to get the most from men. Even if her roomie Carol chooses to be a lesbian, surely that doesn't mean that she should live in poverty as a spinster. According to Capote, some of the best-kept women in New York were actually lesbians:

**PLAYBOY:** Holly Golightly alludes to her onetime Lesbian roommate and obliquely expresses a sexual interest in other women. Was Holly a Lesbian?

**CAPOTE:** Let's leave Holly out of it. It's a well-known fact that *most* prostitutes are Lesbians—at least 80 percent of them, in any case. And so are a great many of the models and showgirls in New York; just off the top of my head, I can think of three top professional models who are Lesbians. Of course, there's a Lesbian component in every woman, but what intrigues me is the heterosexual male's fascination with Lesbians. I find it extraordinary that so many men I know consider Lesbian women exciting and attractive; among their most treasured erotic dreams is the idea of going to bed with two Lesbians.[1]

So while Joan doesn't seem to have an enlightened view of homosexuality, she does seem to have only the best intentions for Carol. But like Golightly, Joan, of course, abandons her roommate to find her own sort of happiness. Though Joan's vision of contentment is more domestic than Holly's, it is equally as elusive.

1. Eric Norden, "Playboy Interview: Truman Capote (1968)," in *Truman Capote: Conversations* edited by M. Thomas Inge (Jackson, Miss.: University Press of Mississippi, 1987), 142.

THEY WORSHIPPED AT THE SHRINE OF PASSION

# TWILIGHT WOMEN

by Les Scott

B156

35¢

K

THE STORY OF
A STRANGE
LOVE CULT
AND ITS SECRET
RITES!

# SALLY DRAPER **AND THE L-WORD**

The night before Don leaves on his overnight trip to Baltimore, Betty tells him that Sally used a hammer to break the clasp on his valise. She offhandedly remarks that Sally has "taken to your tools like a little lesbian."

Was such flip use of the word *lesbian* at all common in the early 1960s? Well, taking into account Betty's background at Bryn Mawr, one of the Seven Sisters schools rather known for its lesbian proclivities, we can assume Betty knows from lesbians.

Additionally, between 1955 and 1969 more than two thousand books were published about "lesbianism." But most of it was ten-cent smut sold in corner drugstores, train stations, bus stops, and newsstands. Code words such as *strange, twilight, queer,* and *third sex* were used in place of *lesbian.* The cover art was, well, erotic. Not surprisingly, these lesbian pulps were largely written by men and were marketed directly to men.

Betty's comment was decidedly brash, but it seems rooted in her dorm days. Particularly because Betty had that sharper, decisive edge in her voice, we can assume that she believes she has firsthand knowledge of "the odd girl out" and therefore has some author-ity on the subject. But her comment was certainly provocative and packed with mysterious implications.

# RELAX, IT'S LIGHT-UP TIME:
# NOTES ON SALVATORE ROMANO[1]
## BY MATT GALLAWAY

"Look at you, Gidget—still trying to fill out that bikini?" asks Salvatore Romano as he walks into Don Draper's office in the first episode of season one and spots Don exercising his pecs with a chest expander. It's a telling first line, not only for its reference to the early 1960s beach movies starring pure-as-the-driven-snow Annette Funicello and Frankie Avalon, but also for the flamboyant manner in which Sal delivers it, so that—but for the lack of winking irony—we could easily imagine it coming from the mouth of a campy drag queen like Charles Busch (who three decades later would mine the same material for *Psycho Beach Party*) or Lady Bunny.

"Summer's coming." Don shrugs, more nonplussed than threatened. In 1960, the camp aesthetic had yet to penetrate the mainstream—Susan Sontag would not publish her famous essay until 1964[2]—and all Don cares about, at least as far as Sal is concerned, is business. Without further ado, Sal unveils his latest concept for the Lucky Strike campaign: an illustration of a bare-chested male model (a neighbor, he somewhat skeevily informs Don while caressing the image) above which can be seen the word *Relax* and below which is a cigarette carton with a red dot.

While Don is unimpressed and requests the addition of a

---

1. Entry by novelist Matt Gallaway.

2. "The essence of Camp is its love of the unnatural: of artifice and exaggeration," Sontag writes. "It is *one* way of seeing the world . . . not in terms of beauty, but in terms of the degree of artifice, of stylization. . . . The hallmark of Camp is the spirit of extravagance. Camp is a woman walking around in a dress made of three million feathers. . . . Camp proposes a comic vision of the world. But not a bitter or polemical comedy . . . not all homosexuals have Camp taste. But homosexuals, by and large, constitute the vanguard—and the most articulate audience—of Camp . . . Homosexuals have pinned their integration into society on promoting the aesthetic sense. Camp is a solvent of morality. It neutralizes moral indignation, sponsors playfulness" ("Notes on 'Camp,'" in *Against Interpretation: Essays* [New York: Farrar, Straus and Giroux, 1966]). This final dynamic is one we see repeatedly played out in the relationship between Sal and Don, who—at least until his business interests are threatened—seems generally amused by Sal and forgiving of his campy (i.e., effeminate, exaggerated) demeanor.

girlfriend, using a real model—a suggestion to which Sal readily agrees with a degree of panting, adolescent exuberance that seems to belie a lack of real experience. We are already in on Sal's secret, even as we wonder to what degree, if any, he has yet to acknowledge it himself. The imperative to relax is particularly fitting here; lifted from an actual Lucky Strike ad campaign from the 1950s— "Relax, it's light-up time . . ."—but divorced of context, the word serves more to reference a mantra in the impending sexual revolution, culminating in the hit song of the same name by Frankie Goes to Hollywood.

At the end of this first scene—in response to an idea (again, in the context of the cigarette campaign) about a societal death wish postulated by a researcher who has joined them in Don's office— Sal gives us an even more definitive glimpse into the closeted depths in which he resides when he smugly says, "So we're supposed to believe that people are living one way and secretly thinking the exact opposite? That's ridiculous." Sal's Freudian slips are often a source of comic relief for the viewer, even as those in the immediate vicinity remain perplexed or fearful (in the case of his wife, after he marries in Season Two). When Sal joins Ken, Paul, and Harry for Pete's bachelor party at a strip joint, he nods to a brunette vixen after she says how much she loves the place because "it's hot, loud, and filled with men" and he responds "I know what you mean," almost batting his eyelids, endearingly oblivious to what we understand is a truer statement than he would like anyone to believe.

Watching Sal over the next two seasons, we are often torn between a sympathetic wish that he would come clean—he's so hapless!—and a vague loathing when he does not. We see him lusting after various men (notably Ken Cosgrove, who writes a short story he shares with Sal about a gold violin that will not play music) but never taking action. We often get the sense that he's happiest

when someone like Don tells him exactly what to do, but given that this is not the way Don (or for that matter, the world) operates, Sal flounders, squandering every opportunity to make significant changes. To be fair, the challenges Sal confronts are complex: in addition to the heterosexual and homosexual worlds between which he remains trapped, he's the only Italian (or "ethnic") executive at Sterling Cooper, and his skills as an illustrator place him in a dying breed as advertising moves increasingly toward photographic and broadcast imagery.

Sadly, though not unaware of these currents and eager to adapt, Sal lacks the strength or vision to ever place himself above the mercy of others. In this respect, he can be contrasted with Andy Warhol, another (homosexual, Catholic) illustrator from the period who in 1960—sensing the same shifting winds on Madison Avenue—dramatically altered his career trajectory. Having built a career over the previous decade drawing whimsical shoes and other illustrations for magazines, Andy decided to become a fine artist; after a series of his male nude torso drawings were rejected by art galleries, he turned to pop art, and became acclaimed after his first opening in 1962.

This is obviously not Sal's path. "You're loud, but you're shy," says a (male) client to Sal later in season one in the course of making a proposition to take him back to his hotel. Sal, who seems more terrified than ever—although of exactly what remains unclear—quickly withdraws his hand and leaves the restaurant. Samuel Delany, in his memoir *The Motion of Light in Water*, offers some insight into Sal's quandary, notably describing a "nearly absolutely sanctioned public silence" with respect to the discussion of anything at variance with the predominating model of heterosexuality.[3] If on the one hand it's understandable that Sal—the son of

3. Samuel Delany, *The Motion of Light in Water: Sex and Science Fiction Writing in the East Village, 1957–1965* (Minneapolis: University of Minnesota Press, 2004), 176.

Italian Catholic immigrants—is extremely reluctant to engage in this discussion, much less to take action, the city was at the same time fairly seething with opportunity for same-sex encounters, as Delany also describes in vivid detail, ranging from the completely anonymous (movie theaters, parks, trucks, subway "johns") to the more traditional bars and hotels (which operated more or less openly by buying "protection" from the police). Describing the trucks at the end of Christopher Street on the West Side, Delany writes that "from about nine in the evening on, between thirty-five and a hundred fifty (on weekends) men were slipping through and between and in and out of the trailers, some to watch, but most to participate in, numberless silent sexual acts, till morning began to wipe night from above the Hudson, to dim the stars, to blue the oily water."[4]

Delany asserts that to witness such activity—which "flew in the face of that whole fifties image"—was that "there was a popula-tion . . . not of hundreds, not of thousands, but rather of millions of gay men, and that history had, actively and already, created whole galleries of institutions, good and bad, to accommodate our sex . . . and any suggestion of that totality, even in such a form as Saturday night at the baths, was frightening to those of us who'd had no suggestion of it before—no matter how sophisticated our literary encounters with Petronius and Gide, no matter what un-derstanding we had reached with our wives."[5] So perhaps this (or a premonition of this) is what really frightens Sal, who—as we have seen in his work—is the opposite of revolutionary. A more duplici-tous, practical man—like Don—presumably could live his married life while having sex with men on the side, but Sal is too earnest for

---

4. Ibid., 121.

5. Ibid., 174.

that, which helps to explain why we like him, despite his ongoing overriding displays of weakness.

But as time passes, events contrive to push Sal closer to the abyss. There is the bellhop on a business trip to Baltimore, where he finally succumbs to what is presumably his first kiss with a man, and would have almost certainly been more had it not been for a fire alarm in the hotel. (From the fire escape, Don witnesses the bellhop leaving Sal's room, and on the plane home obliquely references this, but merely advises Sal to "limit his exposure.") Then there is Sal's decision to rebuff the advances of Lee Garner Jr.—the Lucky Strike client—which seals his fate, at least as far as Sterling Cooper is concerned. As Don says to Sal, nothing stands in the way of a $25 million client. In his final speech to Sal, Don mutters something about his frustration with "you people." Like so much concerning Sal, the meaning is ambiguous: is Don referring to his subordinates, who don't know how to keep a client happy, or is he taking a stab at homosexuals, given what he knows about Sal? I tend to think—at least from Don's perspective—the answer lies closer to the former; if Don was so virulently homophobic, he could have acted against Sal much earlier. Moreover, Don has established himself as a man who disdains the overtly misogynistic antics of his cohorts, which are often only one step removed from those of the homophobic variety.

Whatever Don's intent, we are left with the image of Sal phoning his wife from what appears to be a city park—the notorious Rambles of Central Park, perhaps, but with a telephone booth—surrounded by a group of men dressed in campy leather outfits of the sort that identify them as homosexuals in the parlance of the time. When Sal professes his love to Kitty, it sounds like the thinnest thread, one about to be snapped, leaving him to go places that to this point he has only imagined.

# WEIGHING SINS IN THE STATE OF NEW YORK: DIVORCE

As was relayed to Betty by a gray-faced lawyer, the state of New York did *not* want her to get a divorce! The only legal grounds for divorce in 1963 was adultery, which had to be proved in open court, with one of the spouses testifying to the dalliances of the other while a judge, lawyer, and stenographer bear witness. What you see in the picture is a wife testifying in divorce court while her husband looks on. Nevertheless, at the time, unhappy couples were pushing matrimonial law along—one disillusioned alimony case at a time. The social stigma toward divorce did not dissipate until the tail end of the 1960s.[1]

This exchange from the 1960 Paul Newman film *From the Terrace* between an adulterer and a priest reflected the mainstream attitude toward divorce:

**ALFRED EATON:** What if I don't want to save my marriage?

**JAMES DUNCAN MACHARDIE:** Then we've failed. Then you'll have failed, Eaton. Divorce is a damnable thing. It violates good order. It's a threat to good order.

**ALFRED:** Isn't it just possible that infidelity might be grounds for a divorce?

**JAMES:** There are no grounds for divorce. And if you want my personal theology, infidelity is the lesser sin. I will do anything in my power to prevent a divorce.

**ALFRED:** Including condoning infidelity?

**JAMES:** I consider your word condone disrespectful. I condone none of it. The problem of infidelity is between a husband and wife and God. The problem of divorce concerns the whole

---

1. Fourteen percent of white women who married in the 1940s were divorced. A single generation later, almost fifty percent of married couples that were wed in the late sixties and early seventies have already divorced.

Wife testifying against her husband in a divorce hearing.

of civilization. What is marriage? An exchange of vows, a contract.

Now while this movie was not favorable to MacHardie's character, it reveals the dominant attitude at the time—divorce was considered a greater transgression than adultery. So the hostility and suspicion that is dealt out to divorcée Helen Bishop by the squadron of Ossining housewives is understandable. To be a divorced woman meant you had willfully cheated or testified to your husband's dalliances in court, and in either case failed to maintain your vows, an unsettling notion for any wife—especially for an unhappily married woman saddled with the expectation of a lifelong commitment.

Abortion "client" being taken out of a raided apartment.

# BETTY'S CHOICE

Francine offers Betty (tepid) congratulations upon hearing that she's expecting a third baby. "It's not a good time," Betty says over and over until Francine eventually offers to give her the name of a doctor who specializes in this sort of problem.

Her manners prevent her from giving it a name, but Betty's desire is clear: She wants an abortion. Beyond any emotional or moral difficulty—which cannot be discounted with a Main Line nice girl like Betty—finding a doctor willing to perform the procedure would have been a humiliating affair.

In *The Fifties: A Women's Oral History,* an upper-middle-class housewife named Pam Dillon tells Brett Harvey her story:

When I got pregnant for the fifth time, I wanted an abortion. I went to my ob/gyn—I never shopped around for an obstetrician, I went to this guy because he was eminent and came highly recommended. He always treated me like a child, but I was used to that. But when I went to him to ask for an abortion, he said, "Oh nonsense, you'll love having a fifth child. After all, you've *got* four, what's one more?" I was enraged. And desperate. Somebody told me about a doctor in New Jersey who was doing abortions. So I went out there, found this place all by myself, sat in the waiting room for about half an hour. When I told the doctor I wanted an abortion he just stared at me and said, "I don't know what we're going to do about that." Finally my husband's sister, who worked in a hospital, found me a doctor who gave me an abortion. There was just no way in hell I could have handled a fifth child.[1]

1. Brett Harvey, *The Fifties: A Women's Oral History* (New York: HarperCollins, 1993), 94.

A married woman of means like Betty had a shimmer of a shot getting a legal abortion in 1963. She could apply to the Mount Sinai obstetrics panel for a "therapeutic abortion." She would require the recommendation of a psychiatrist that her life would be in danger if she were to carry her baby to term—due to threats of suicide or utter mental collapse. Then, two consultants from the ob/gyn field would have to be consulted, and one would have to testify before the abortion panel. Affluent women could manipulate the system and get approval—in fact, one out of four abortions approved by the panel in 1958 were given to married women. Nevertheless, this sort of legalized procedure was increasingly rare.

The other option for Betty would be an illegal abortion from a doctor or nurse who was willing to risk jail and ruin for performing the procedure.

The price often influenced the quality. Caitlin Flanagan outlined the potential differences (and similarities) of criminal abortions across class lines:

> Reports a woman who got pregnant while a student at Barnard in the 1930s: "The actual abortion was comfortable, clean, the absolute tops." On the other hand, here's a description of an abortion the actress Margot Kidder had as an eighteen-year-old in the mid-1960s. Her boyfriend, John, made the arrangements, "all done with great secrecy and a great sense of evil and sordidness"; the couple were told to check in to a certain hotel room where the abortionist, a woman, would meet them. After gaining their assurance that they would never go to a hospital if something went wrong, she began the procedure.[2]

---

2. Caitlin Flanagan, "The Sanguine Sex," *Atlantic*, May 2000, 110.

Kidder then underwent a painful and messy abortion that involved a tube forcibly pushed through her cervix so Lysol could be pumped into her uterus.

Or Betty could have had the baby and proceeded with her original plan to separate from Don. But, according to Brett Harvey, "single motherhood was not a viable choice if you were white and middle-class: the stigma was simply too crippling to live with. If you were black, your family and community might treat you with more compassion, but your life was irrevocably changed."[3]

Surveying her options, Betty decided to reconcile with Don and have the baby. But then again, for Betty Draper, there weren't many options available.

---

3. Harvey, *The Fifties*, 22.

# BETTY IN STIRRUPS, DON IN WAITING

Betts endured a nightmare at the hands of a Ratchedesque obstetrics nurse while Don had his feet up in the cozy solarium. It wasn't until the late 1970s that men were regularly allowed in the delivery room. Until then, men's role in a pregnancy, as far as the medical establishment was concerned, ended at conception. Before then it was argued in the pages of women's magazines and medical journals that men would contaminate the delivery room, both physically and psychologically. Doctors didn't want to encourage the "prurient interests" of men.[1] According to obstetrics historian Judith Walzer Leavitt, men's opinions were changing. In 1949 new father Dale Clark wrote of his experience: "It's about time for all husbands—the whole crowd in the waiting lounge—to grab hatchets and chop through the partition"[2] separating them from their laboring wives.

The key to allowing men into the delivery room was held by French obstetrician Dr. Fernand Lamaze.

Lamaze classes became popular in the United States during the late 1960s. This was due in part to the burgeoning sense of egalitarianism, thanks to the civil rights movement, and the publication of Marjorie Karmel's book *Thank You, Dr. Lamaze*. Lamaze is more than a breathing exercise, it's an ideology that emphasizes the organic nature of childbirth. It advocates that women should feel as relaxed as possible during labor and are entitled to a birth without medical intervention.

---

1. Richard K. Reed, *Birthing Fathers: The Transformation of Men in American Rites of Birth* (New Brunswick, N.J.: Rutgers University Press, 2005), 77.

2. Judith Walzer Leavitt, *Make Room for Daddy: The Journey from Waiting Room to Birthing Room* (Chapel Hill: University of North Carolina Press, 2009), 49.

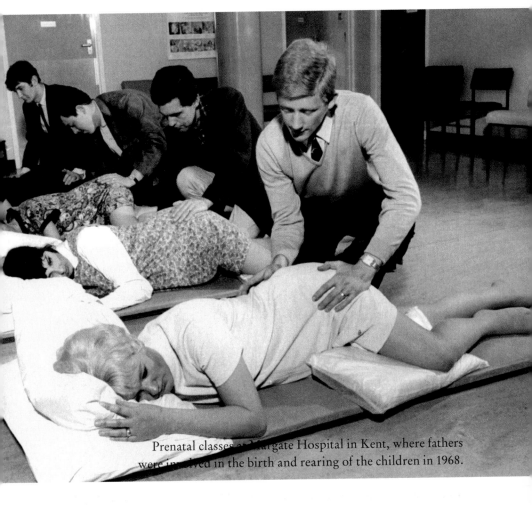

Prenatal classes at Margate Hospital in Kent, where fathers were involved in the birth and rearing of the children in 1968.

The Lamaze breathing technique also requires a partner (originally a midwife). During the civil rights and women's liberation movements, more and more men signed up for classes with their ladies and were eventually seen as helpful partners rather than meddlesome outsiders.

# 5

# SMOKING, DRINKING, DRUGGING

Tell them to wait another 15 minutes—
I'm just enjoying a

# CHURCHMAN'S No. 1

CHURCHMAN'S No. 1, THE 15-MINUTE CIGARETTE

C31F

## "PUFFING WHILE PREGNANT"

Francine innocently and comically smokes cigarettes and downs wine by the bottle throughout her pregnancy. Betty furiously lights up one (filtered) smoke after another as her belly swells out to *here* with baby Gene. Didn't they *know* any better? Actually, because of men like Don, probably not.

Though one of their favorite magazines, *Reader's Digest,* had been sounding the alarm since 1924, and had made huge, splashy headlines with their 1952 "Cancer by the Carton" article, most women assumed cigarettes were pretty safe and not that harmful. The occasional magazine story was nothing compared to the onslaught of advertising featuring doctors in white coats and stethoscopes nullifying the health complaints.

A Kool's illustration shows a stork delivering a "bundle of joy," which is not a baby but a pack of their cigarettes. L&M's were "just what the doctor ordered," and "eminent medical authorities" recognized Philip Morris—though, of course, "more doctors smoke Camels than any other cigarettes."

Marlboro ads even suggested smoking would make you a better, more patient mother. They featured a pouting baby reminding his mom to light up a Marlboro "before you scold me."

As more damning studies emerged, some doctors understood the gravity of the nifty habit and recommended that their patients quit. Most didn't, in denial because they were smokers themselves. While about 40 percent of the adult population smoked in 1964, more than 53 percent of doctors were slaves to the habit.

The early studies of the fifties and sixties were focusing on the link between tobacco and lung cancer, not the effects of smoking on a fetus. It wasn't until the 1970s that the trend of smoking pregnant women would lose steam, eventually becoming an egregious social faux pas viewed by some as a sign of neglect. In 1989, 19.5 percent of births were to women who smoked during their pregnancy; this number would drop to 10.2 percent in 2004.

It wasn't until 1966 that every pack Betty would smoke would carry a dire warning from the surgeon general.

# ALWAYS BE SMOKING:
# WHY DON WON'T QUIT[1] BY ALEX BALK

Don's physician knows he's being bullshitted. Don dodges and lowballs until the doctor insists, "I'm trying to help you here." Don cops to five drinks a day but hedges on the rest. Before Don can say anything else, the physician fills in the next answer: "And two packs a day but you're cutting down?"

The dangers of smoking had been creeping into public consciousness for some years before Don's checkup in 1962. *Reader's Digest,* the highest-circulation magazine in the United States at the time, ran its lengthy piece "Cancer by the Carton" that stubbed cigarette sales for years. The health fears raised by that story were something that Don knew quite well.

So did every thinking man, to cadge a phrase from one high-profile tobacco sales pitch of the time. "It frightens me to think of what is going to happen in another decade when our present smoking habits catch up with us," one cardiovascular doctor was quoted as saying in the breakthrough article. "Already, lung cancer has achieved pandemic proportions . . . it is significant that the sharp increase in lung cancer is almost exactly proportional to the increase in cigarette sales. I am convinced that the heavy smoker will develop lung cancer—unless heart disease or some other sickness claims him earlier."

But even if Don's doctor compelled him to give up smoking for the sake of his health, it's unlikely a guy like Don would ever quit. Don would never have put down a cigarette for the same reasons some of us won't do it nearly a half century later in an atmosphere that to him would have been unthinkably more hostile to those who like to light up. Doing a pack or two a day nowadays is a

---

1. Writer and blogger Alex Balk is founding coeditor of *The Awl.*

cultural proxy for slovenliness, poverty, or just pure, unadulterated evil. Beginning in the early 1960s and mounting through today, the scientific evidence against smoking grows so overwhelming that it requires not just an act of faith by which to partake in it, but an active denial of what has become, for good reason, the conventional wisdom. We know that smoking will probably kill us. Even if we are some of the lucky few who escape the deadliest medical tolls the inhalation of tar and nicotine takes on the body, we are the subjects of scorn and derision; aspersions are cast on our intelligence, our elegance, and, of course, the way we smell.

Don, however, came up at a time when smoking, in spite of the first public scoldings, was still irretrievably associated with sophistication, sensuality, and romance (think of Paul Henreid lighting two cigarettes at the same time and then passing one to Bette Davis in *Now, Voyager*). Don smoked and continued smoking because of two compelling motives: One, he was surely addicted to nicotine. Second are the myriad reasons that, with all the scientific and cultural cues, so many men continue to smoke even today. There are a couple of heady postulations, including the idea that despite demonization, smoking has endured. The act of drawing hot smoke into your lungs still retains a touch of manliness, of strength and unspoken prowess. That might as well be a dictionary definition of the words *Don Draper.*

Don didn't have to worry as much about generalized masculine insecurity and drooping social status as modern males do. And that leads us to one theory why men, in spite of all we know, still tar their lungs—i.e., that smoking's sadly reduced status makes the act of engagement even that much more rugged and rebellious. Another credible suggestion involves the idea that men as a whole are pretty much stupider than women and thus more likely to engage in risky behavior.

I recently had an appointment with a physician for a general checkup. I had not been to a doctor in years, so the practitioner in question was new to me and I to him. We went through the inventory of my habits so he might better assess the damage I was doing to myself. I had decided ahead of time to be completely honest, and so I was: about my drinking (Herculean), the amount of exercise I took (none other than the completely necessary or utterly inadvertent), and whether or not I smoked (I do, usually a pack a day). There is no history of lung cancer in my family, and I am of an age where what used to be muscle is making its inevitable devolution into fat, but guess which of these behaviors was the one with which he was most concerned? Actually, don't guess; if you've been to a doctor yourself, or seen any health PSAs on television or in the papers, or have simply observed what we as a society have deemed to be the activity most deserving of scorn in this era, you already know. He was appalled by my smoking.

All of these theories have much to recommend themselves, but I would also put forth this: We live in an age where the idea of masculinity is, if not the overblown bleating of "under threat," in rapid transition. With women overtaking men as a majority of the workforce (an effect that the most recent recession both accelerated and probably made permanent), a majority of those attending and completing degrees in institutions of higher learning, and as those who will eventually be the bigger financial earner in relationships, men begin to wonder what their place is in this world, and how they can rationalize their instincts toward domination when all the facts are so starkly stacked against them. And thus, smoking, with its primal feelings of the mastery of fire, the control of one's own destiny, and the very male delusion that one can look in the face of Death and say, "Here I am, give it your best shot." The men who continue to smoke do so because it is one of the few avenues of total power left to them in an age of confusion and change.

Also? It feels pretty fucking great. Let's not forget that part of it. I know it. And so did Don.

# DAZE OF WINE AND ROSES: OFF TO REHAB

Moments before a meeting with Samsonite, a drunk Sterling Cooper executive, Freddy Rumsen, wets his pants. Will he become a Madison Avenue legend, as Peggy suggests, or a cautionary tale to future ad men about the destructive nature of alcoholism?

Freddy is fired in a halfhearted intervention by Don and Roger, delivered over double martinis. He is given the option to dry out and return, but Freddy begins to list other agencies he might apply to, cities he might move to, rather than give up drinking to stay at Sterling Cooper. Don and Roger nod in approval.

"Your alcoholics may include some of your brightest stars," David Ogilvy wrote in a section devoted to the subject in his book *Ogilvy on Advertising*. "The problem is to *identify* them, protected as they always are by their secretaries and colleagues." Ogilvy suggests a surprise dinner meeting with the afflicted employee and his wife, a plea for his family and health, and a reservation at a rehab center the next day. "Most alcoholics agree to go," Ogilvy counsels. "It takes a week for them to dry out, and another four weeks to rehabilitate them. On returning home, they must go to daily meetings of Alcoholics Anonymous for at least a year."[1]

In 1956 the American Medical Association categorized alcoholism as a disease rather than depravity caused by loose morals and a penchant for sinning. Freddy would no longer be considered a deviant, but an addict. Adding to a public, frank discussion about alcoholism that excluded notions of piety was one of the most popular films of 1963, *Days of Wine and Roses,* which raked in $4.3 million and earned Jack Lemmon an Academy Award nomination. Lemmon starred as a PR man who, with his lovely

---

1. David Ogilvy, *Ogilvy on Advertising* (New York: Vintage, 1985), 53–54.

young wife, descends into alcoholism. The movie is part morality tale, part promo for Alcoholics Anonymous, part horror film. Lemmon's character eventually gets clean with the help of AA, but his wife, whom he introduced to drink, remains addicted.

The most striking scene is his collapse in a sanitarium. Such deviant behavior could have instilled disgust rather than compassion in Pete Campbell, who justifies tattling on Freddy by asking Peggy, "Why do you feel bad for him? Those people always blame their problems on society. He did it to himself. Those people have no self-control."

Before Betty Ford made rehab a socially acceptable if not chic place to go, before celebrities broadcast their experience of "getting clean" on television, there was Hazelden. Roger encourages Freddy to take "the cure" at Hazelden, a secluded 217-acre farm outside of Minneapolis. This was the first rehab facility in America, started by some members of Alcoholics Anonymous. By 1960 the center was using a multidisciplinary approach to cure alcoholism, employing medical doctors along with psychologists as well as former alcoholics as counselors. According to Roger, his podiatrist had gone there and it changed his life: "He only drinks beer now."

# "TAKE A PILL AND LIE DOWN": PSYCHIATRY IN THE 1960S

Don can do nothing but roll his eyes at psychiatry.

Roger believes that it's just a 1960s "candy pink stove" for girls.

Don asks Roger how long his teen daughter had been seeing a shrink; Roger denies she ever did (even though he had confessed it at dinner over drinks a couple of days earlier). Roger pours himself a scotch, exhales, and says: "You know what? I am very comfortable with my mind, thoughts clean and unclean, loving, and . . . the opposite of that. But I am not a woman." He sighs. "And I think it behooves any man to toss all female troubles into the hands of a stranger."

Don responds, "We had one head shrinker in the army, a gossip, busting in on other people's thoughts."

"Hasn't changed much, just costs more," Roger says.

Don answers, "And you just can't shoot at them."


**THE FAD STATUS** of psychiatry that Roger referred to was thanks in part to the powerful nexus of altruism and entrepreneurialism coming out of World War II. Public sentiment toward psychiatry thawed and more humane treatment for psychological "deviants" were adopted as war veterans came home from the front injured and mentally addled. Additionally, the postwar economic boom allowed a lower rung of the professional class, such as psychiatrists, to establish private practices in the suburbs. The momentum kept up, and by the early 1960s systematic change swept through the profession: open-door policies, informal admissions, and the burgeoning prescription of psychotropic drugs.

The prime petitioners for psychiatric treatment at the time were socially mobile young housewives. The cohort, per medical convention, were prone to "emotional episodes" such as depression, neurosis, and suicide.[1] One of the most popular psychotropic drugs prescribed to woebegone housewives was phenobarbital, classified as a hypnotic and barbiturate and used as a catch-all remedy for nerves, anxiety, and depression. The pill depresses brain function, reduces breathing, slows the heart rate, and decreases body temperature. Though it was a powerful sedative, thanks to its popularity, it gained a casual household status like today's Xanax or Zoloft. Now it's mostly used to treat seizures in epilepsy patients.

When a phenobarbital prescription didn't cure the emotional episodes of a housewife, other methods of anxiety relief could be prescribed. For instance, after being on phenobarbital for years to treat her anxiety, Minnie Cooper of Boyle Heights, California, a mother of twin daughters whose husband worked as a steel salesman, was told by her psychiatrist that she should perhaps have another child in order to occupy her thoughts and energies. One year later in 1950, she gave birth to my dad. Somehow that didn't seem to cure her anxiety.

---

1. Richard E. Gordon and Katherine Gordon, "Psychiatric Challenges of the 1960s," *International Journal of Social Psychiatry* 10, no. 3 (1964): 223–31.

# DÉCOR

# THE DRAPERS' DÉCOR: INSIDE 42 BULLET PARK ROAD

When you think of the prototypical 1960s home you might think of something space-agey, streamlined, geometric, and monochromatic. Or maybe something shaggy and accented with dingbats. But how wrong you would be.

Most suburban homes in the early midcentury still clung to a colonial revival décor. Colonial revival (a less frilly but still traditional) style was considered stately, high-class, and warm. There would be some flip accents, sure (note Betty's textiles: the curtains and blankets are more on the whimsical side, like the giant afghan on the couch).

In 1924, an article entitled "The Charming Dutch Colonial Type" suggested:

> [I]n the Colonial home, old-fashioned furniture will give a charming atmosphere. Large four-poster beds, higher than the usual bed, fresh dotted Swiss curtains, brightly colored rag rugs, either round or oval shape, will go far toward fitting up an ideal but simple bedroom. Small legged tables or chairs, a little desk, painted or lacquered, may be placed in

odd corners of a room of Colonial type, to brighten it up perceptibly. Every piece of furniture which is bought for the house should be appropriate, not only in being Colonial, but also by being well proportioned to the size of each room. Many homes are utterly ruined when furnished improperly. If the owner would bear in mind that a good idea is to try to make the furnishings eclipse the architecture and even the grounds, he would never fail in having a beautiful and picturesque dwelling. Simplicity, but good judgment is the keynote.

Most homes built in the early 1900s, like the Drapers', were relatively stripped down and lacked the eighteenth-century flourishes of older homes. To achieve the traditional colonial style, designers and homemakers were instructed to "paint the walls a soft tint such as ivory, parchment, green, or apricot." Additional touches such as small period details, fabric, lighting, and small colonial-style furniture, including tilt-top tables and rush-seated chairs, were encouraged.

# PLANTATIONS **AND PARK AVE.**

In the mid-1970s, artist Marcel Broodthaers began work on an installation that he called *Décor: The Conquest*. He placed objects in two separate rooms; each depicted a different century. One room was suggestive of the nineteenth, all lined with stiff, ornate wooden chairs, palm trees, and rusting cannons placed on tidy squares of grass. The other room, outfitted with aqua blue patio furniture, machine guns, and streamlined bookshelves, was presumably meant to reflect the tastes of the modern era. Let's go inside two other starkly different interiors: Roger Sterling's country club bash and Joan Holloway's Manhattan digs.

In the twilight of the Eisenhower era, it's easy to understand Roger's desire for a Southern gentry–style party. What greater way to unapologetically revel in the wealth of the withering patrician class than to throw a Derby party? "My Old Kentucky Home," the theme of Roger's Derby party and the name of the ditty he crooned while in blackface, was the state's official song. The opulence of a Derby party—no matter how tastefully done—is impossible to untangle from a racist "cultural heritage."

> *The sun shines bright in the old Kentucky home,*
> *'Tis summer, the darkies are gay;*
> *The corn-top's ripe and the meadow's in the bloom,*
> *While the birds make music all the day.*
> *The young folks roll on the little cabin floor,*
> *All merry, all happy and bright;*
> *By 'n' by Hard Times comes a-knocking at the door,*
> *Then my old Kentucky home, goodnight.*

A typical Derby party, like Roger's, features a towering circus tent filled with gaudy rose bouquets, men in ye-olde-style floppy bow ties, their dates in garish floral dresses, all pretending as though they were members of an extinct breed of Southern aristocracy.

And though the racial attitudes in the days of flannel suits and TV dinners had evolved enough to make Don Draper grimace at Roger's minstrel act, it was likely the Derby party's nostalgia for plantation excess that made a Dust Bowl farmhand like Don uneasy.

Well, to hell with all that. Toss away the mint julep and let's go sip martinis in Joan's cozy midcentury apartment. Joan lives in a world about five rungs down the class ladder from Roger, but she still manages to stay chic and thoroughly modern. Her apartment has the Draper touch—*Dorothy* Draper, Manhattan's sometime top interior designer until her death in 1969. The color scheme and décor here are lifted directly from a Dot Draper tear sheet. "Dorothy used vibrant, 'splashy' colors in never-before-seen combinations, such as aubergine and pink with a 'splash' of chartreuse and a touch of turquoise blue, or, one of her favorite combinations—'dull' white and 'shiny' black. Her signature 'cabbage rose' chintz, paired with bold stripes; her

elaborate and ornate plaster designs and moldings—over doors, on walls and ceilings . . . all contributed to dramatic design often referred to as 'the Draper touch.' "[1]

Additionally, Joan's insistence on proper hostess etiquette comes from Dot herself. In 1941, Draper's book *Entertaining Is Fun! How to Be a Popular Hostess* was a huge best-seller. Together, Dot and Joan have a loose and playful sense of décor. Clash the colors, hang an antique mirror, and serve the booze in dingbat-patterned glasses. Be exuberant but never gaudy.

Based on the data load provided by their two interiors, Roger could be a lost cause for the future—washed out by the young folks rolling on the little cabin floor. And questions about Joan's ability to adapt to what we modern viewers know is the coming cultural shift remain unanswered—but perhaps there is hope in her couch cushions.

1. History of the Interior Design House of Dorothy Draper & Company, Inc.

# THE JAPONISME OF BERT COOPER'S OFFICE

Let's spend some time in Bert Cooper's office. Surely you've noticed the Asian themes. Tall, black-lacquered chairs with looping flourishes; cranes on rice paper; ceramic dragon lamps. The décor is called Japonisme, a French term that translates into Japanism. There was a heightened interest in Japanese graphic arts, textiles, and fashion at the turn of the century (an offshoot of the Western love affair with art nouveau). The ornate and excruciatingly detailed art from Japan, according to the Metropolitan Museum of Art in New York, "depicted simple, transitory, everyday subjects from 'the floating world' [that] could be presented in appealingly decorative ways."

By the 1910s, Japanese graphic arts and textiles were all the rage in the States.[1] It would make sense that someone like Bert, older than the rest, would design his office with regal furnishings from Japan. Not that Bert is out of touch, he just has older tastes—more mature than the Dorothy Draper turquoise wave that was rolling through Manhattan.

On one of his grass-covered walls, next to the Rothko, is the erotic woodcut of a naked woman with her legs wrapped around a virile octopus: its suckers are latched onto her nipples, shoulders, and neck, while its beak is pressed against her middle. Another smaller octopus kisses her open mouth. The work is *The Dream of the Fisherman's Wife* by Japanese artist Hokusai (circa 1820). Far from being lewd, the cut reflects the Japanese artistic tradition of depicting a playful attitude toward sexuality (which anyone who

---

1. Europeans saw their first formal exhibition of Japanese arts and crafts when Japan took a pavilion at the Exposition universelle d'Art et d'Industrie in 1867. Shortly thereafter, shiploads of Asian bric-a-brac—including fans, kimonos, lacquers, bronzes, and silks—began pouring into England and France. By the early 1900s the style went Stateside (Sarah J. Oshinsky, "Exoticism in the Decorative Arts," in *Heilbrunn Timeline of Art History* [New York: Metropolitan Museum of Art, 2004]).

works in advertising must have). It is a celebrated piece that has been reworked by a number of artists since the nineteenth century.

Behind Bert's desk is a cream ceramic lamp with a regal foo dragon at its base. Foo is a traditional Chinese style that depicts lions, dragons, and other regal beasts in an active pose, bug-eyed and snarling.[2]

I asked an interior design associate, Max Humphrey, who has beautiful turquoise foo lamps in his home, why are they so lovely? He responded, "They're classic. I don't need to explain good taste."

---

2. When Don wanders around in the eccentric desert palace ("The Jet Set"), what should pop up on the shelf but a pair of burgundy foo dogs! A writer and former lackey of a hip furniture store, Johnny Dale, sent me this note about the significance of the foo:

Cooper's office is blatantly Japanese-themed; could the appearance of the foo dog here be intended to draw a parallel between Cooper and the menacing Felliniesque aristocrats of this episode? And if so, what? I guess a case could be made that Cooper is the show's representation of idly bohemian old money, in which case he certainly has a lot in common with Joy's family and friends, and this foo dog would be a reminder to Don that no matter how high he rises in the world he'll always be new money, a lowborn man who made his fortune by working.

# SHOGUNS OF STERLING COOPER

"Japan" is the explanation Bert Cooper offers his British bosses for why they must strip down to their socks to enter his office.

Lurking in the corner of his Japanese-themed workplace is a full samurai suit, likely from the Edo period (1603 to 1868). Beyond just decorative choice, it's easy to see why a war vet and art connoisseur like Bert would feel a spiritual kinship with the samurai. More than just professional warriors, the Japanese samurai were also cultural visionaries, a sort of military aristocracy.[1]

In feudal Japan, the samurai code—personal, societal, and political—was to maintain the delicate balance of *bun* and *bu*, or culture and arms. In his introduction to *The Art of the Samurai* exhibition catalog (2009), Hosokawa Morihiro wrote:

> Culture and arms are like the two wings of a bird. Just as it is impossible to fly with one wing missing, if you have culture but no arms, people will slight you without fear, while if you have arms but no culture, people will be alienated by fear. Therefore, when you learn and practice both culture and arms, you demonstrate both authority and generosity, so people are friendly but also intimidated, and they will be obedient.

Perhaps to secure his own ranking as a man of equal civility, prowess, and taste, Lane Pryce propped up a buffed medieval knight's suit to stand guard in his office. Whatever their actual motivations may be, it's clear that empire-building does come with some marvelous accessories.

---

1. The samurai arose from warrior bands formed to protect the Japanese imperial capital in Kyoto. They gained importance and political power through the Heian period (794–1185) and instituted a military government (shogunate) in the Kamakura period (1185–1333).

# THE WHITE HOUSE TOUR: JACKIE KENNEDY MESMERIZES THE NATION

Joan stops necking with her young man of the moment to plead, "You have to see this."

"No I don't," he insists and continues to paw her.

Joan's eyes stay wide open and wander back to the television set, where Jackie Kennedy's gracious figure leads CBS correspondent Charles Collingwood on a tour of the White House, softly reciting facts about paintings and chairs. Joan was riveted by what Theodore H. White would later call "the most successful nonfiction show" ever created by CBS.[1]

Joan, Salvatore, Betty, and Francine weren't the only ones tuning in. Its immense success would lead to a shift among viewer demographics as the networks scrambled to add more female-oriented programming in the evenings.

On February 14, 1962, *A Tour of the White House with Mrs. John F. Kennedy* aired on CBS and NBC, and was seen by three of four TV viewers. ABC rebroadcast the show four nights later and it was later syndicated in fifty countries. Network news documentaries were a popular genre of television in the 1960s. The *Tour* was radical, though, as Jackie was the first female narrator to air during prime time, expertly describing art and furnishings as Collingwood and the audience hung on her every word.

Jackie had an addictive love of decorating and redecorating. She was a perfectionist who would often redo a room several times until it was exactly right. Joseph Karitas, a housepainter, tells the story of repainting a blue room beige in the East Wing and being interrupted by President Kennedy, "barefooted, big cigar in his

---

1. *Jacqueline Kennedy: The White House Years* (New York: Metropolitan Museum of Art. 2001), 8.

mouth, magazine in his hand. He said, 'What in the world? She's doing it over already?' "[2]

Jackie revamped a tired, shabby White House into a "historical document of cultural life in the United States." She trashed cheap, imitation furniture and replaced it with luscious French pieces that preceded 1802, the year the house was built. Personally overseeing the remodel, Jackie shows her exuberance in her memos to the chief steward of the White House:

> "Mr. West. I so like the rug, but we are short on dollars and I am ENRAGED at everyone trying to gyp the White House. Tell him if he gives it he can get a tax deduction and photo in our book—if not—goodbye!"[3]

Similar network documentaries with the likes of Elizabeth Taylor and Sophia Loren would later air. These attempts at formulaically reproducing the ratings magic of a nation held captive by the First Lady's charm would gain some success, but none would ever be as successful as the 1962 White House *Tour*.

2. Carl Sferrazza Anthony, *The Kennedy White House* (New York: Touchstone, 2001), 65.

3. *Jacqueline Kennedy,* 7.

# SUBURBAN ROCOCO:
# DRAPER RESIDENCE IN REGENCY

Throwing open her arms, a matronly interior designer introduces Don to his new living room as Betty waits anxiously on the sidelines. The new décor is a dulled regency style with Eastern flourishes, more sophisticated than the colonial revival décor but still muted and trendy. The designer introduces each piece to Don with a special emphasis on high-end labels.

"It's hard to believe this now," Former *House & Garden* editor in chief Dominique Browning said in a recent interview, "but labels were all-important then. Everybody knew *exactly* what it meant that you purchased X or Y, and these magazines, along with professional decorators, played a crucial role in guiding insecure housewives through these decisions."[1]

Here's what they got:

- A chinoiserie breakfront, the French name for "Chinese style" cabinet. Sometimes this style is called Chinese regency. Chinoiserie became all the rage in eighteenth-century France when Louis XIV decorated Versailles with new, fanciful European interpretations of Chinese styles. It had a steady resurgence in twentieth-century design.
- A Japanese-influenced Dunbar couch. A low-slung and brass-footed couch was a staple of midcentury design. I assume the "Japan" twists are the sharp-angled armrests.
- Dupioni silk drapes. This is the shiny silk that's also used to make prom dresses. It's a shimmering silk that is created by

---

1. Kate Bolick, "The Fainting Couch for Best Supporting Actor," doubleX.com, September 28, 2009.

weaving silk threads of two different colors into a pattern
that seems to change colors as the silk is moved around in
different light.

✕ Murano vases. These are glass blown Venetian style;
transparent.

✕ Drexel end table. Drexel was a furniture company a rung up
the class ladder from Crate & Barrel in its day.

It seems as though the world is tugging away at Don Draper's individuality one thread at a time. Now Don's own hearth, the place
where he puts up his feet and thinks about the majestic Mohawk
nation, has been invaded by a home designer who has undoubtedly
put the same "modern chinoiserie" design into the homes of hundreds of other stylish couples.

# 7

## LITERATURE

**LADY CHATTERLEY'S LOVER**
D. H. LAWRENCE

# STENO POOL BOOK CLUB:
## *LADY CHATTERLEY'S LOVER*

*Lady Chatterley's Lover* has the unique history of being privately published, banned, pirated, expurgated, republished, and the cause of a groundbreaking obscenity trial.

The notorious novel by D. H. Lawrence was originally published in 1928. Critics dismissed it as laughably provocative or just pure smut. Beyond containing some naughty Anglo-Saxon slang (one rhymes with *duck* and the other with *runt*), it was the themes of the work—sexual liberation, the crushing heel of marriage, and securing one's individuality through sexual relationships—that made European and American censors squirm.

In 1959, thirty years after Lawrence's death, the novel was re-released and was an instant sensation. Within a year *Lady Chatterley's Lover* sold two million copies, outselling even the Bible that year.

From the dog-eared copy of that naughty book floating around the Sterling Cooper steno pool:

And softly, with that marvelous swoon-like caress of his hand in pure soft desire, softly he stroked the silky slope of her loins, down, down between her soft warm buttocks, coming nearer and nearer to the very quick of her. And she felt him like a flame of desire, yet tender, and she felt herself melting in the flame. She let herself go into it. She yielded with a quiver that was like death, she went all open to him.

Penguin publishers was then accused of breaking obscenity laws in England by publishing the book. The prosecution argued that there was no artistic merit in distributing such morally dubious prose and that the novel was just pornography. To defend the artistic merits of the piece, Dame Rebecca West, E. M. Forster, and Richard Hoggart took the stand.

The prosecution failed to make a substantial case against the novel, and at one point the prosecution counsel asked the jury: "Is it a book that you would even wish your wife or your servants to read?"

Or your steno pool?!

# THE UNSENTIMENTAL MEN OF AYN RAND

Bert puts some socioeconomic theory into practice when he hands Don an unexpected bonus. Befuddled and slightly alarmed, Don begins to stammer in lieu of clearly expressing gratitude. Bert gave Don an extra $2,500 because of Ayn Rand. He tells Don that he believes, as Rand does, that the ideal life is one that "has resolved personal worth into exchange value."

"When you hit forty, you realize you've met or seen every kind of person there is," Bert says. "And I know what kind you are, because I believe we are alike. . . . By that I mean you are a productive

ATLAS SHRUGGED
Ayn Rand

and reasonable man and in the end completely self-interested. It's strength. We are different. Unsentimental about all the people who depend on our hard work."

Bert then encourages Don to take two bucks out of his mondo bonus and pick up a copy of Rand's 1957 best-selling novel *Atlas Shrugged*. For the uninitiated, the primary lesson of *Atlas* is individual selfishness must be put first, else a society will collapse. In Rand's dyspeptic future, parasitic autocrats and businessmen hoard a nation's wealth by collectivizing land and industry. Society's greatest innovators and thinkers refuse to contribute to the economy and engage in a "strike of the mind." When the state fights back, oil fields are set ablaze and trains derailed by striking industrialists. Society quickly disintegrates.

Rand's intention was to champion the ethos of unfettered "rational self-interest." "I work for nothing but my own profit—which I make by selling a product they need to men who are willing and able to buy it." This was the mantra of the mind strikers, whose creativity, according to Rand, was more important to society than physical labor. If their creativity was not rewarded, Rand concluded, our progress would halt.

So, accordingly, Bert greases the wheels of Sterling Cooper's progress by awarding the head of Creative some cold cash.

# OSSINING: CHEEVER COUNTRY[1]
## BY ANGELA SERRATORE

Often called the "Chekhov of suburbia," in his short stories John Cheever explores the tension between the public facade and internal strife of midcentury bedroom community dwellers. In Cheever's Ossining, home to the Drapers, upper-middle-class husbands catch the Metro North to and from the city and never miss cocktail hour or an opportunity to dramatize the stultifying effects of the 'burbs on the inner creative.

Stories like "The Swimmer," "The Five-Forty-Eight," and "The Country Husband" are all about upper-middle-class husbands and fathers beaten down by routine and unable to express basic human desires. Himself a secret bisexual, not-so-secret alcoholic, and fabricator of an upper-crust background (his mother ran a gift shop on the South Shore of Massachusetts; his father lost the family fortune and drank heavily), Cheever hit his stride in the late 1940s, counting among his fans the cantankerous Harold Ross, editor in chief of the *New Yorker*, a magazine that served as the primary vehicle for his short stories until his death in 1982, though his early 1960s work for *Atlantic Monthly* would have made him a peer of our own Ken Cosgrove.

Perhaps Cheever's most famous story, "The Swimmer" encapsulates his attempts to paint suburbia as a place that provides its men and women (but mostly men) with material wealth at the expense of spiritual happiness. Our hero, Neddy Merrill, decides to reclaim his vitality by navigating across his unnamed Westchester hamlet, swimming pool by swimming pool, "breathing deeply,

---

1. Entry by Angela Serratore, a writer and historian in suburban Los Angeles.

stertorously, as if he could gulp into his lungs the components of that moment, the heat of the sun, the intenseness of his pleasure." By story's end, the sun has gone down and Neddy finds himself locked out of his own seemingly abandoned home, with no clear memory of how it came to be that way.

Critics often refer to Westchester as "Cheever country," but perhaps "Draper country" might be more apt?

Bullet Park John Cheever

# BETTY'S BATHTUB READING: *THE GROUP*

So, where did Betty get her chutzpah—or as a WASP-y Main Line "brat" of her ilk might call it, the moxie—to declare D-day on Don? Henry Francis? Betty Friedan? Or was it all that time soaking with Mary McCarthy in the bathtub?

McCarthy's 1963 bestseller was a fictional account of the post-Vassar lives of "nice" girls trying to reconcile their adolescent ambitions with their largely unsatisfying adult lives in the 1930s. The novel's literary reputation is that it was ahead of its time for its frank depiction of women's stunted happiness when faced with a society that valued them most for their domestic abilities above all else. Beyond the proto-feminist critique, the book also offers a good bit of satire for the astute reader. McCarthy's unconventionally vicious, knifelike descriptions of her heroines provide much black comedy, with their "lack of self-awareness, their bad judgment, their blind hypocrisy," according to the *London Review of Books*. "Honest readers may conclude that they are not so very different themselves; when the feeling of superiority wears off, satire occasionally gives rise to sympathy."

Here's a passage from *The Group* that very well may have resonated with our white-nosed Betty. Kay, a college grad in an unhappy marriage to a creative type named Harold, fantasizes about taking the train to Reno:

She had loved him at first, she reckoned, but he had tormented her so long with his elusiveness that she did not know, honestly, now whether she even liked him. If she had been sure of him, she might have found out. But things had never stood still long enough for her to decide. It sometimes struck her

Mary McCarthy

that Harold would not let her be sure of him for fear of losing his attraction: it was a lesson he had learned in some handbook, the way he had learned about those multiplication tables. But Kay could have told him that he would have been far more attractive to her if she could have trusted him.[1]

Still, Betty's matrimonial discord may not have arisen from McCarthy's provocative fiction. According to Norman Mailer's sneering review of the novel, "These pissout characters with their cultivated banalities, their lack of variety or ambition, perversion, simple greed or depth of feeling, their indifference to the bedrock of a collective novel—the large social events of the season or decade which gave impetus to conceiving the book in such a way. Yes, our Mary's a sneak. Like any First Lady she disapproves of unseemly ambition, and yet she is trying a novel which is all but impossible to bring off in a big way."[2]

So, maybe this wasn't a flaming match thrown onto Betty's marital tinderbox. And to confuse matters more, the character that most resembles Betty Draper is Elinor, the lesbian who jets off to Europe for most of the book. Overall, in terms of liberating her from domestic oppression, Betty and *The Group* is something closer to a factory worker picking up *The Wealth of Nations* instead of *The Communist Manifesto*.

---

1. Mary McCarthy, *The Group* (New York: Harvest Books, 1991), 414.

2. Norman Mailer, "The Mary McCarthy Case," *New York Review of Books* 1, no. 4 (October 17, 1963).

# PHILIP ROTH IN BULLET PARK[1]
## BY NATASHA SIMONS

Red-eyed with grief over her grandfather's death, Sally Draper hugs the floor as she watches the first televised self-immolation of a Buddhist monk. A spate of these suicides by fire will ensue in reaction to the ongoing war in Vietnam. In Buddhism and other Eastern warrior cultures, the practice of self-immolation is simultaneously a form of denouncement and of devotion.

Sally's being glued to the television in the wake of a death and her parents' inability to comfort her signifies an ongoing distancing of Sally from her surroundings, and, more important, the 1950s atmosphere still pervading her home. Her witnessing such a tragic event at an early age will no doubt have an effect on her consciousness, especially in a time of grief. Another fictional character of some infamy witnessed, and became obsessed by, the very same Buddhist self-immolation: Merry Levov, from Philip Roth's *American Pastoral*.

> She [Merry] watched in total silence, as still as the monk at the center of the flames, and afterward she would say nothing; even if he spoke to her, questioned her, she just sat transfixed before that set for minutes on end, her gaze focused somewhere else than on the flickering screen, focused inward— inward where the coherence and the certainty were supposed to be, where everything she did not know was initiating a gigantic upheaval, where nothing that registered would ever fade away. . . .[2]

---

1. Entry by Natasha Simons, who likes Philip Roth and televised national tragedies.

2. Philip Roth, *American Pastoral* (New York: Vintage, 1998), 156.

If Sally Draper had been just a few years older she could be going the way of a violent sixties radical like Merry. This fiery scene could be Sally's baptism into political consciousness by fire.

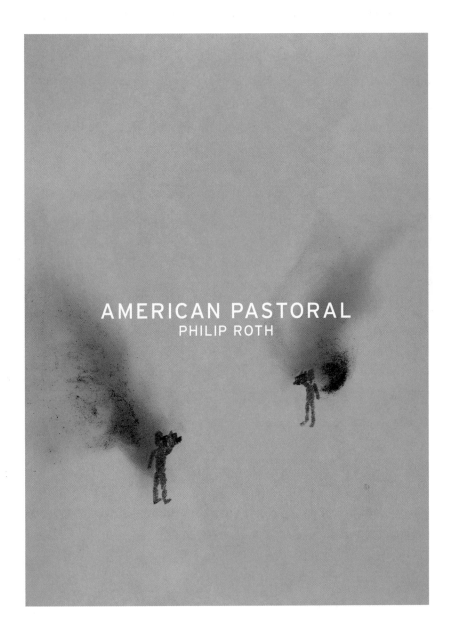

# AN INTIMATE YELL: FRANK O'HARA

A scraggly-haired hipster at a bar tells Don Draper he probably wouldn't like Frank O'Hara's *Meditations in an Emergency*. What a fool! O'Hara's poetry is tailor-made for someone like Don; the thematic focuses are the indulgences, nightmares, and paradoxes of modern life (all refracted through the grungy kaleidoscope of Manhattan)—the same subjects that trigger a lot of Don's brooding introspection.

The central concern for both men is best illustrated through the myth of Sisyphus: a man condemned to the futile task of rolling a rock up the mountain just to have it perpetually roll back down again. This is what Albert Camus described as that conflict between what we want from existence (such as meaning, order, or reasons) and what the universe gives us. With the rise of the mechanized world and the advent of the bomb, modern man's task of rolling the rock up the mountain seems even more absurd. This seems to be the kind of emergency O'Hara refers to in the title of his collection and the same cause of dread for Don.

But for both men, the indifference of the universe and its emptiness can be neutralized by living the most varied life as possible, which translates into an exuberance for romance, coffee, cigarettes, drink, and sex.

O'Hara's work was largely confessional and unashamed. He's regarded as a founding member of the New York School during the midfifties, a cluster of writers defined by their loose style and passionate—though often panicked—prose, which was often autobiographical.

In the collection's titular poem published in 1961, O'Hara wrote,

*I am the least difficult of men. All I want is boundless love.*

Before the confessional style of the New York School, the can-
onized poets of the previous generation, like T. S. Eliot and Ezra
Pound, advocated a depersonalized aesthetic, arguing that poetry
had to be elevated out of its smelly, corporeal form. Eliot's masterpiece "The Waste Land," for instance, is a studied collage of Latin
phrases, obscure mythological conceits, and scraps from ancient
poets. The footnotes on "The Waste Land" encompass about 500
years of Western history—and that's just for one poem!

O'Hara and his contemporaries struggled to yank poetry out
of the classroom. "You just go on your nerve," O'Hara said of his
poetry. "If someone's chasing you down the street with a knife you
just run, you don't turn around and shout, 'Give it up! I was a track
star for Mineola Prep.' " As for technical aspects of poetry, O'Hara
said, "that's just common sense: if you're going to buy a pair of
pants you want them to be tight enough so everyone will want to
go to bed with you."[1]

Originally from Baltimore, O'Hara did a stint in the navy and
enrolled at Harvard on the GI Bill. He roomed with illustrator
Edward Gorey while tinkering with a novel and studying music.
When he arrived in New York in 1951, he started working as ticket
taker at the Museum of Modern Art. O'Hara wrote poems on napkins and at parties; he allegedly wrote the entirety of the collection
*Lunch Poems* at a counter during his lunch break from his fellow-
ship program at the museum. When came it came time to publish,
O'Hara would have to spend hours around his apartment digging

---

1 Frank O'Hara, "Personism: A Manifesto," *Collected Poems of Frank O'Hara* (Berkeley: University of California Press, 1995), 498–99.

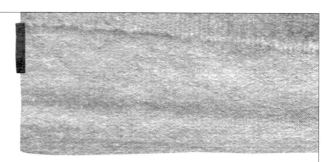

# Meditations
# in an
# Emergency

**Frank O'Hara**

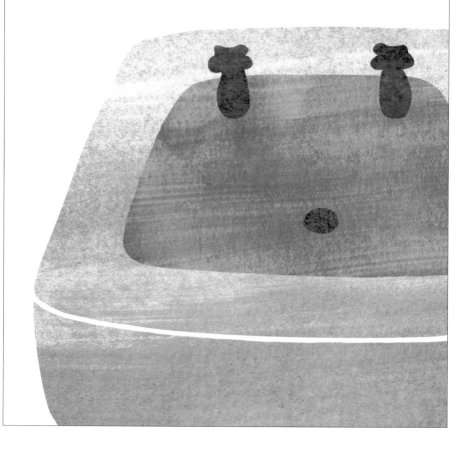

up poems written on scraps and napkins. He was quickly embraced by some of the major luminaries of the avant-garde scene like Willem de Kooning, John Ashbery, Kenneth Koch, and Jasper Johns.

Manhattan in the midcentury, the abstract art scene, the cold war: all served as the monumental backdrop for O'Hara's personalized poetry. A poem for friends who were to be married was published in the *Meditations* collection:

*honeymoon isn't used much in poetry these days*

*and if I give you a bar*
*of Palmolive Soap*
*it would be rather cracker-barrel*
*of me, wouldn't it?*[2]

A trait O'Hara and Don Draper share in common is their deep love of the movies. O'Hara exuberantly embraced lowbrow topics, such as Lana Turner, Coca-Cola, and the common movie house. Can't you just see the smile on Don's face when his eyes rolled over this poem, "To the Film Industry in Crisis"?

*Not you, lean quarterlies and swarthy periodicals*
*with your studious incursions toward the pomposity of ants,*
*nor you, experimental theatre in which Emotive Fruition*
*is wedding Poetic Insight perpetually, nor you,*
*promenading Grand Opera, obvious as an ear (though you*
*are close to my heart), but you, Motion Picture Industry,*
*it's you I love!*[3]

---

2. Frank O'Hara, "For Janice and Kenneth to Voyage," in *Meditations in an Emergency*, 49.

3. Frank O'Hara, "To the Film Industry in Crisis," in ibid., 3.

The poem we hear Don read as we watch him drop a copy of *Meditations* in a mailbox on his desolate suburban block is named after the revered Soviet poet Vladimir Mayakovsky. Like O'Hara's, Mayakovsky's poetry encompassed themes of diminution, renewal, and romance. But after he had suffered through a tumultuous love affair, futility overwhelmed Mayakovsky and he committed suicide in 1930. In his final poem he wrote,

*"the incident dissolved"*
*the love boat smashed up*
*on the dreary routine.*
*I'm through with life*

"There is but one truly serious philosophical problem," Camus wrote of the Sisyphus myth and modern man, "and that is suicide." That quandary permeated modern literature (and Don's recent past with the death of his brother) as well as O'Hara's poetry, especially in "Mayakovsky." The five-part poem begins with a sexual tryst, a ruptured heart, and then O'Hara enters a frigid wasteland of his own:

*Now I am quietly waiting for*
*the catastrophe of my personality*
*to seem beautiful again,*
*and interesting, and modern.*
*The country is grey and*
*brown and white in trees,*
*snows and skies of laughter*
*always diminishing, less funny*
*not just darker, not just grey.*[4]

---

4. Frank O'Hara, "Mayakovsky," in Meditations in an Emergency, 51.

However, at the point where Mayakovsky's "love boat" would crash against the rocks, O'Hara veers and continues on, for reasons generally having to do with the glorious pleasures of mundane treats and rowdy love affairs. It's soothing to read O'Hara, particularly a poem like "Mayakovsky," because it seems to acutely capture the modern mood, the sensation of an atomized heart pounding furiously in a dissolving world.

O'Hara died at the age of forty while vacationing on Fire Island after being struck by a jeep while he and his fellow passengers waited for a beach taxi to be repaired. Inscribed on his gravestone is a line from his poem "In Memory of My Feelings":

*Grace to be born and live as variously as possible.*

# 8

## MOVIES

# THE SEXUAL ALCHEMY OF DON DRAPER

The amalgamation of qualities that makes Don Draper so irresistible can also be found in the greatest male movie stars of the time.

Dark eyes, brown hair, strong jaw, and a faint but permanent look of melancholy—in appearance and biography, Don is an undeniable match for Cary Grant. Grant was born as Archibald Leach, to a mentally ill woman and a working-class pants presser in Bristol, England. He spent years performing as a tumbler with a traveling group of acrobats before he was discovered by Paramount. When Grant eventually appeared on-screen, his style was poised, intelligent, and desirable, but still his mutt past was never fully exorcised, giving his persona enough edge to make him film history's most indelible leading man. Even with his good manners and deference, Grant always seemed to be masking a touch of darkness. Film historian David Thomson wrote of Grant: "The essence of his quality can be put quite simply: he can be attractive and unattractive simultaneously; there is a light and dark side to him but, whichever is dominant, the other creeps into view."[1]

This description is true for Don as well. Don Draper never seems to entirely dispossess himself of Dick Whitman. Don's

---

1. David Thomson, *The New Biographical Dictionary of Film* (New York: Knopf, 2002), 361.

dodgy though concealed past tempers his slickness and enhances his appeal.

Grant, though, was at his best when he was being chased by the alpha starlets of the era. From screwball comedies to suspense thrillers, the great leading ladies—Mae West, Katharine Hepburn, Rita Hayworth, Grace Kelly—all tried to seduce Grant. (Indeed, Don is similarly simpatico with commanding women such as Rachel Menken and Bobbie Barrett.) It's when both men find themselves around aggressive females that they are most desirable. Mae West winked at Grant when she knowingly asked, "Why don't you come up and see me sometime?" Thirty years later, Audrey Hepburn delivered a similar invitation to Grant in *Charade*. "Won't you come in for a minute? I don't bite, you know, unless it's called for."

But here's where Don and Grant part ways. You could rely on Grant to play nice while a woman worked herself up into a lather over his charms. There is a much more forceful quality to Don's sexual charisma. In terms of masculine prowess, Don most resembles Clark Gable. You did not playfully invite Gable in for sex hoping he would be courteous.

Gable's sexual charisma was an open challenge to women. Pauline Kael captured his essence best when she wrote, "Gable got down to brass tacks; his advances were basic, his unspoken question was 'Well, sister, what do you say?' If she said no, she was failing what might almost be nature's test. She'd become overcivilized, afraid of her instincts—afraid of being a woman."

Just think of the scene in the restaurant between Bobbie and Don. Don takes a fistful of Bobbie's hair, slowly pulls her toward the floor, and slides his other hand up her skirt. It's unclear if Bobbie's whimpers are from agony or ecstasy; whether it's what Don is doing under her skirt or her strained back.

The same violent, primal appeal appeared on-screen and off-screen with Gable. Even the toughest of women weren't immune to it: Joan Crawford said being around Gable on set gave her "twinges of sexual urge beyond belief."[2] Looking at the suggestion of force behind both Don and Gable's smiles makes Crawford's confession all too believable.

But then again, Don doesn't spend very much time smiling, does he? He's a little too prone to self-destruction and pessimism ever to be as cavalier as Gable was. Don's constant introspection, his tangle of morals, the calm fatalism that overcomes him when he faces the unknown is trademark Humphrey Bogart, the unlikely sex symbol of so much of film noir that Don no doubt sat through with a knowing admiration for the disillusioned detective played by Bogie. This "intellectual isolation," as described by Thomson, that both Don and Bogart exhibit implies complexity, which at times can be maddening for women (particularly Betty, who one night stares at the back of Don's sleeping frame and asks aloud, "Who is in there?") and, yet, is nonetheless incredibly sexy.

There is a final trait about Don that perhaps only a woman can recognize. Though he rarely flaunts it, there is a sense of safety about Don. It's clear that he has a sturdy, protective embrace. You can see it in his early encounters with Suzanne the schoolteacher. Or when Betty's family is in crisis. Though they are separated, Don insists on traveling with her to her Pennsylvania mansion to run defense against Betty's smarmy brother and wicked stepmom. Later that night, on the floor of her childhood bedroom, we witness one of few instances where Betty sexually advances on Don. Whether it's ancient biology or socialized norms, there is a protection that

---

2. Irving Wallace, Amy Wallace, David Walleschinsky, Sylvia Wallace. *The Intimate Sex Lives of Famous People* (New York: Dell Publishing, 1981), 40.

Don offers that we women want. And who epitomizes the home-steading patriarch better than John Wayne? Not even the most eru-dite, urbane women—like say, Joan Didion—could resist Wayne's bowlegged, virile swagger. In 1965 Didion wrote a diary-style essay about her love for Wayne: "As it happened I did not grow up to be the kind of woman who is the heroine in a Western, and although the men I have known have had many virtues and have taken me to live in many places I have come to love, they have never been John Wayne." Didion echoes the line from Wayne's *War of the Wildcats,* where he tells his young lover that he would build her a house at the bend in the river where the cottonwoods grow. She wrote, "Deep in that part of my heart where the artificial rain forever falls, that is still the line I wait to hear."[3]

---

3. Joan Didion, "John Wayne: A Love Song," *Slouching Towards Bethlehem: Essays* (1968; repr. New York: Farrar, Straus and Giroux, 2008), 30.

# SNOW-COVERED VOLCANO: GRACE KELLY

Grace Kelly is the same archetypal figure as Mrs. Betty Draper: a simmering sexual persona behind a glacial veneer. Just lookswise, she and Birdie have a lot of the same things going on: demure, delicate, with a suggestion of the upper class in all that she did.

Kelly was from money, and while attending a fancy Pennsylvania academy, Ravenhill, she did some modeling with her sisters and appeared in amateur plays. She went to the same dramatic arts

school as Spencer Tracy and Katharine Hepburn. Kelly had a brief and glorious stint in Hollywood: six years. Her regal, locked-jaw style was best exploited under director Alfred Hitchcock. He called her "a snow-covered volcano."

She starred in *Rear Window* and *To Catch a Thief*. The *New Yorker* applauded her virginal beauty and "quiet confidence." She cinched an Oscar for *Country Girl* in 1954.

Then she literally became a princess: Kelly married Prince Rainier of Monaco in 1956. Her official title became Her Serene Highness, the Princess of Monaco, and she spent the second half of her life throwing charity balls and giving out awards to dignitaries and starlets. It was known among those close to Kelly that she was homesick, lonely, and prone to heavy drinking and bouts of depression. She eventually moved out of the palace. Former Washington editor for *Vogue* Sandra McElwaine summed up the grim third act of Kelly's fairy tale: "Kelly found herself ensnared in a splendiferous prison. Bored by enforced retirement and endless protocol, she took an apartment on posh Ave. Foch in Paris, ostensibly to oversee her children's education, but friends considered it [a] separation of sorts."[1]

One day in 1982, while driving her daughter to their country house, Kelly lost control of her car on a hairpin turn and was killed.

---

1. Sandra McElwaine, "Last Role for Princess Grace," dailybeast.com, December 12, 2009.

# ANN-MARGRET FEVER[1] BY CAROL DIEHL

Ann-Margret, then Ann-Margret Olsson, was a few years ahead of me at New Trier High School in the Chicago suburbs. One of three thousand overachievers in a public school that boasted a fully professional theater facility and a faculty sprinkled with Ph.D.s, Ann-Margret was already an icon—a cheerleader and the star of everything. She was dark-haired and beautiful, with a singing voice that could handle any style.

I remember a prom where she sang a jazz song a cappella, holding a room filled with probably a thousand teenagers rapt. But even though her version of "Heat Wave" in the student variety show was so hot my friend Donna's parents walked out, it wasn't her sexiness that stood out—she wasn't provocative at all—but rather her strength and determination. She didn't go out with the high school boys; my ex-husband, who was in a band with her briefly, said that it was because she knew she was destined for greater things.

Fast-forward a couple of years: I'm on vacation somewhere with my parents, watching (I think) the *George Burns Show*, and there's Ann-Margret, completely transformed. Her straight, glossy dark hair is now frizzled and red-blond, she's speaking and singing in an unfamiliar little baby voice, and, like her character in *Viva Las Vegas*, acting all weird and coy. I didn't understand it at the time, but looking back it was one of those coming-of-age moments as I wondered, why would she hide her talents and do this to herself? Why would she allow this to be done to her?

While it might appear today that we've gone overboard with the whole sexual harassment thing, *Mad Men* recalls what it was like to be female before the culture had those constraints—the

---

1. Carol Diehl is an artist, writer, contributing editor to *Art in America,* and author of the blog Art Vent.

high school and college teachers who hit on me and then gave me bad grades, the (two) dentists who would rub themselves against me as they drilled (think of how conveniently the dental chair is situated), doctors who took advantage (how to explain my first gynecological exam to my mother? I didn't), the purchasing agent at Evanston Hospital who literally chased me, the temp, around his desk. Then there was my only corporate job—at Whitney Communications, which owned *Art in America* in the mid to late 1970s—where, among other things, the vice president used to routinely feel my back to see if I was wearing a bra and snap it if I was. That was our world; we took it for granted. Once we discovered we had rights, that we didn't have to put up with this shit, yes, we were angry. What I love about *Mad Men* is that it's not an exaggeration.

# DON'S WEEPIES: *LA NOTTE*[1] BY NATASHA SIMONS

One of the things Don actually admits to, under interrogation by Bobbie Barrett and extreme alcohol intake, is that he likes the movie *La Notte*! Who knew that Don was such a sophisticated aesthete?

*La Notte* was directed by Michelangelo Antonioni (*Story of a Love Affair, Blow-Up*), and it stars a personal favorite actor—and Draper-esque prototype—Marcello Mastroianni. Think James Joyce's *The Dead,* but way more Italian.

There's a focus on memory and the resurgence of the past, on intangible relationships, on wandering through life like sleepwalkers, half alive, half dead. (But keeping with the Italian vibe, there's also dancing.) It's about a man and his wife who engage in flirtations and affairs until the end, when she wakes up one morning and tells him she doesn't love him anymore.

There's a big party scene where Giovanni, the husband, socializes and glad-hands while his wife lingers on the edges of things, there as a trophy, lonely in a crowd of people. The similarity should strike you pretty quickly if you recall Don and Betty at the Kentucky Derby party. It doesn't end there. Giovanni is a restrained man-child, someone who has everything he could want but can't manage to connect to the happiness those trappings ostensibly entail. His indecisiveness, his recklessness, and his creative frustration (he is a writer) remind us of our own leading man.

So why does farm-bred Don love foreign film so much? Well, the educated consumer, middle-class, with tendencies toward art, totally gave up on American cinema around the 1950s and into the 1960s. American 1950s cinema was maudlin dreck. It was all

---

1. Entry by Natasha Simons, *Mad Men* researcher and lover of weeping middle-class men.

gimmicks and wide-screen and teenage idols romping around—
not serious enough for a man of Don's taste. This is when imports
took off, and in particular, Italian cinema boomed. The neorealist
movement, referred to by some as "male weepies," really got an
American audience interested. The French Nouvelle Vague and the
British working-class kitchen sink movement was also right around
this time, and provided a foreign escape route from the American
chaff of the day.

# FRITZ LANG PRESENTS PENN STATION

The Madison Square Garden corporation wants to tear down Penn Station—a neoclassical architectural marvel—for a stadium.

This upsets Sterling Cooper's Paul Kinsey: "Fifteen stories. Vaulted ceilings. Pink Milford granite columns. I don't think it's crazy to be attached to a Beaux Arts masterpiece through which Teddy Roosevelt came and went. . . . Do you know where the greatest Roman ruins are? They're in Greece. Spain. Because the Romans tore theirs all down. They took apart the Colosseum to build their outhouses."

The scheming vice president of Madison Square Garden

chastises him for being just like that no-goodnik Ada Louise Huxtable. Huxtable is an award-winning architecture critic who is still elegantly trashing developers over at the *Wall Street Journal*.

In 1963, when the war for Penn Station was lost, Huxtable wrote a rich and wry farewell for the *New York Times*: "Any city gets what it admires, will pay for, and, ultimately, deserves. Even when we had Penn Station, we couldn't afford to keep it clean. We want and deserve tin-can architecture in a tinhorn culture. And we will probably be judged not by the monuments we build but by those we have destroyed."

Don's remark that any public dissent to the destruction would just be a formality suggests that the new Penn Station was an idea drawn up by the rich and imposed on a public unable—or unwilling—to fight back.

When the ads for the refashioned Penn Station do finally get discussed—no thanks to Paul—Pete Campbell says they apparently look like something "right out of *Metropolis*."

Who knew Pete appreciated German Expressionist cinema? *Metropolis* is the touchstone of the genre. It depicts a monochromatic landscape dominated by diamond-etched angles and imposing infrastructures. *Metropolis* is a dystopian vision of an overmechanized world, wherein an overpopulated city is at the mercy of businessmen and technocrats who dwell in sky-piercing towers. Throughout the film, the proletariat, as Paul might say, are overshadowed both literally and figuratively by the city's architecture.

# *THE MISFITS*: THEY EAT HORSES, DON'T THEY?

Wet dog food flavors came in beef, liver, chicken, and horsemeat. They eat horses, don't they? Yes, "they" do! "They" nowadays is just Europeans and dogs—not Americans. Beyond any sort of animal rights advocacy, there's an American cultural taboo about the human consumption of horsemeat, even though it's perfectly legal. The horse, it seems, is too much a sentimental character in American mythology to be edible—even for our pets. But touting the savory flavors of equine hash was once a selling point. That was before *The Misfits* was released in 1961.

Bert Cooper and the dog food heiress cite *The Misfits* as the reason behind the public backlash against horsemeat and collapsing sales of a potential new client. The film was meant to be a sweeping western with a dazzling cast: Marilyn Monroe, Clark Gable, and Montgomery Clift, under the direction of John Huston, with a script by Arthur Miller. These beautiful screen stars rope and ride the elegant ponies. (Before the ponies are sent to the slaughterhouse for dog food.) It's not a great movie—making titans of the screen seem like ordinary western folk is tough business, even for John Huston. But it's a fascinating cultural landmark for bringing all those fading talents together.

David Thomson, the fabulous critic, wrote of the picture: "[I]t follows one of director John's Huston's favorite subjects: horses. In turn, the best stuff of the picture involves the actors trying to rope and tame wild horses on silvery flats outside of Reno, Nevada. Huston, at least, could look at a horse and see just the wild four-footed miracle. Yet somehow this aching movie is driven to see the horses as symbols of lost purity in America."[1]

American purity dislikes being dragged into the dog bowl.

---

1. David Thomson, *Have You Seen . . . ?: A Personal Introduction to 1,000 Films* (New York: Knopf, 2008), 559.

# JOAN IN *THE APARTMENT*

With his wife and daughter away for Labor Day weekend, Roger Sterling wants to wine and dine his mistress, Joan. He points out that with most of Manhattan's mothers and children at the beach, he and Joan can see any show and sit in the middle of any restaurant—naked, if they so desire.

Unfortunately for Roger, Joan's got other ideas.

"How about a movie? Have you seen *The Apartment*?" she taunts him, waiting for an opportunity to describe the misfortune of Fran Kubelik, a congenial elevator operator played by Shirley MacLaine, who sleeps with the married men in her office building. "The way those men treated that poor girl, handing her around like a tray of canapés?" When Roger says nothing, Joan snaps, "She tried to commit suicide."

This exchange comes on the heels of a hotel room tryst, in which Roger suggests that Joan get her own apartment so they could stop sneaking around.

"Don't you like things the way they are?" Joan asks while putting on her earrings.

"Are you kidding?" Roger responds. "This has been the best year of my life. Do you have any idea how unhappy I was before I met you? I was thinking of leaving my wife."

RELEASED IN 1960, Billy Wilder's *The Apartment* likely sparked similar spats between professional men and the women who loved them (no, not their wives—the *other* women who loved them). Jack Lemmon stars as C. C. Baxter, a hapless middle manager whose apartment is considered community property by his bosses: they use the pad to conduct extramarital liaisons. The suicide attempt

to which Joan refers comes after MacLaine's Kubelik, object of affection for Lemmon's Baxter, is faced with the grim realization that Baxter's boss Sheldrake, played by Fred MacMurray, is, despite his apparent interest in her, cold, rational, and unlikely to leave his wife. Sound like anyone we know?

As film critic David Thomson points out, "In hindsight, I have the impression that *The Apartment* feels very sour, with an unconvincing happy ending tacked on. Its world (like that of *Psycho*) is unrelievedly bleak—Sheldrake, for instance, is a very cold-blooded fellow."[1]

Roger attempts to convince Joan that she's not like Fran and he's not like Sheldrake, and succeeds in making her laugh, but the damage has already been done. Unmasking the glamour of the workplace affair, *The Apartment*'s cynical take on the relationships between powerful men and beautiful young women forces all Joans to question the motives, feelings, and intentions of all Rogers.

---

1. David Thomson, *Have You Seen . . . ?: A Personal Introduction to 1,000 Films* (New York: Knopf, 2008), 43.

# 9

**IN PROGRESS**

A group of beatniks sit in an apartment (24 Cornelia Street),
New York, NY, December 5, 1959.

# DON IN THE VILLAGE: BOHEMIANS V. INDIFFERENT UNIVERSE

There is a vibrant culture clash in Midge's smoke-choked Greenwich Village apartment: the man in the gray flannel suit versus the barefoot bohemians; the establishment versus the emergent counterculture; or was it just one system of symbols versus another, something like the Rebel Brand versus the Mainstream Brand?

Here's a snatch from the confrontation that took place between Don and the self-styled nonconformists:

**MAN IN FEZ HAT:** Dig—ad man with a heart. Toothpaste doesn't solve anything. Dacron sure as hell won't bring back those ten dead kids in Biloxi.[1]

**DON:** Neither will buying some Tokay wine and leaning up against a wall in Grand Central pretending you're a vagrant.

**MAN IN FEZ HAT:** Do you know what it's like to watch all you ants go into your hive? I wipe my ass with the *Wall Street Journal*. . . . Look at you—satisfied, dreaming up jingles for soap flakes and spot remover, telling yourself you're free.

---

1. Dacron is a trademark polyester fabric, a chemical product used in the mass manufacture of textiles, clothing, and beverage and food containers. It had first been developed in Great Britain before World War II but then was taken up by the American company Du Pont in 1954. Like nylon, it was easily washed, quick-drying, and shrink-proof. It was advertised to consumers as the new miracle product that never needed ironing. Ads pictured salesmen in Dacron suits diving into swimming pools or standing under showers fully clothed ("Textiles: Enter Dacron" *Time*, May 21, 1951).

**DON:** My God. Stop talking. Make something of yourself.

**ROY:** Like you? You make the lie. You invent want. You're for them . . . not us.

**DON:** Well, I hate to break it to you, but there is no big lie. There is no system. The universe is indifferent.

**MAN IN FEZ HAT:** Man, why'd you have to say that?

This idea of counterculture, the Us v. Them dichotomy has always existed in Western civilization (see Supreme Court case *Jesus v. Romans*), but this specific bohemian scorn against "the ad man" was fomented specifically during the 1960s.

It is so easy to take Don's side in this moment. History more or less proves him right. (Plus, it's difficult to feel sympathy for a pigeon-chested twentysomething in a peasant shirt when he is standing next to Don Draper.) The political changes that defined the sixties and seventies came about through a combination of disciplined political action—not music festivals, consumer trends, and fashion choices.

In the view of Midge's glassy-eyed party guests, society had become overrun with lies and propaganda thanks to hyperconsumption fueled by advertising. The world was soiled by injustices (like Biloxi), and yet people were told freedom was to be found in washing machines and Cadillacs.[2] "The system," then, was considered a huge swindle of

---

2. The Man in the Fez Hat may be referring to a terrible race riot that broke out in Biloxi, Mississippi, on April 24, 1960, as 40 to 50 African Americans attempted to swim at a whites-only beach in a peaceful protest. The civil rights activists were bloodily beaten by a mob of angry whites with chains, blackjacks, and baseball bats. By the end of the night, two white men and eight black men had been shot. It would be eight years before the Mississippi Gulf Coast was ruled as public property and all races were allowed access to the beach. Here is one harrowing firsthand description of the riots.

    Carney said the number of police officers was scarce, but he remembers one officer's words to the large mob.

    "The civil rights had been signed into law and he told the crowd, 'Legally, I can't get them off, but you can,'" said Carney. "And when he said that, those people headed for that beach like a stampede."

    The Biloxi beach became a battleground. The men say police stood by and watched as people were beaten with bricks, chains and baseball bats.

    "I saw a black man who had been kicked so much in the face that his eyes had literally turned green," said Carney.

    (Elise Roberts, "Remembering the Biloxi Wade-ins.")

images and symbols that repressed individualism and truth. The way to rebel was to renounce symbols of greed, discipline, and uniformity.

The rub? This was done by adopting a whole new system of symbols: sandals instead of Florsheims, jeans instead of chinos, a bare midriff to outrage the mothers who taught their daughters to be polite and find husbands, or even a Paul Kinsey–style beard to broadcast the notion that you and your face will not be constricted by the tyranny of disposable razors!

However, Don affirms there is no system: the universe does not care what kind of shoes you do or don't wear; it will continue to spin mercilessly, unmoved by human turmoil (no one knows this better than a Dust Bowl refugee like Dick Whitman). So the counterculture that Midge's buddies adopted was supposed to build a new world on individual freedom. Now we have the benefit of being forty years in the future and seeing that this project of theirs did not work so well: The system of hyperconsumerism was not staved off by bearded men in ironic fez hats, it's still thriving and it has absorbed into it every possible strain of "counter" markets.

So then, where does that leave Don? Don is also in revolt. But is his brand of rebellion any more or else authentic than the bohos in the corner? After all, this conversation is being had in the apartment of Don's mistress. Don revels in the same kind of hedonism and rule breaking to satisfy his individuality as the dope smokers do. The guy shows up an hour late every day, bucks at authority, and has joyless sex with powerful women for what reason exactly? To shake off that creeping alienation that comes from living in a world of well-disguised lies?

Well, at least his feet are clean when he does it.

# SUN SETS ON THE EISENHOWER ERA: WORLD'S FAIR, NEW YORK, 1964

Amid discussion at Sterling Cooper about tearing down Penn Station for the Madison Square Garden arena, the ad agency's participation in the upcoming 1964 World's Fair is mentioned. Don argues that the arena is their ticket into the fair. He tells his would-be client that "New York City is in decay" and needs something new.

The fair was a holdover from the nineteenth-century tradition of giant international expositions. The fairs held in Chicago (1893) and in New York (1939) were considered two definitive moments in America's ascension to global power by demonstration of enormous gains in manufacturing and innovation. The 1964 fair was meant to be a formal display of our way of life to the rest of the world: stability, adaptability, and social tranquility through tremendous technological development. The themes for the fair were "Man's Achievement on a Shrinking Globe in an Expanding Universe" and "Peace through Understanding." Instead of serving as a boastful anthem for American dominance, the fair was a death rattle of the Eisenhower establishment.

It was a total flop. After the first season, the fair was running 25 percent below expected attendance (70 million over two years) and ran at a $10 million deficit. Mismanagement (and possible fraud) led investors to lose ninety cents on the dollar. Fair organizers and investors took tight, bureaucratic control and drove away any chance of spontaneity or exuberance.

The fair, it's believed, failed to attract crowds because organizers banned construction of a midway. A midway built adjacent to the fairgrounds was a kind of honky-tonk amusement park, offering fair attendees fast rides, cheap games, tent shows, and other titillating lowbrow pleasures. But a carnival where different classes and races could mingle and whet their appetites for crude entertainment was deemed undignified. New York's financial leaders would have no hurly-burly show sullying their trade exposition. In place of games, firecrackers, and Ferris wheels, there were only staid, museumlike buildings that served as containers of things to be displayed or purchased.

The progress being made in Detroit and Los Angeles was well represented: Ford debuted the Mustang, and Disney's prototype for "It's a Small World" and its animatronic dolls were a hit. But New York sank into a grungy malaise that would last for decades.

# "WHEN YOU LOOK AT IT, YOU DO FEEL SOMETHING": ROTHKO

How do you describe a Rothko? Ghostly rectangles hovering on top of a field of bold color? Queerly interdependent, delicate shapes with shifting hues? None of that seems to capture the transfixing power of Mark Rothko's monumental works. Ken Cosgrove's description is pretty accurate, though: "When you look at it, you *do* feel something."

But the charge most commonly brought against modern artists like Rothko is that their work was far too elusive. Their work was purposefully without form simply to be contrary to thousands of years of artistic convention. Like Peggy's replacement, Jane, says when she sees the looming burgundy painting in Bert's office, "Oh, it's just smudgy squares."

Abstract art, like that of Rothko and the modernists, was not just a rebellion against the conventions and restrictions of the current art; their work also embodied the radical advances made in mathematics and science at the turn of the twentieth century. Atomic energy, relativity, and quantum physics offered artists altered concepts of time, space, and vision.

You can blame molecular theory most of all: the discovery that solid objects were comprised of negative and positive electrons bouncing off one another and in a constant state of gyration challenged (if not destroyed) the assumption that sight and touch offered the highest level of verification of reality. The artist and the writer were subjected to the notion that the environment, which they had been meticulously attempting to reproduce, had been turned on its head.

Some critics have interpreted modernist work as a furious embrace of secular nihilism: a generation of artists so disillusioned by

the modern that they abandoned all forms of structure. But I join the school of thought that believes the modernists were attempting to reach an ultimate level of authenticity in their work by circumventing earthly forms in order to present something universal and emotional (that's pretty idealistic!).

In the June 13, 1943, edition of the *New York Times,* Rothko, together with Adolph Gottlieb and Barnett Newman, published the following brief manifesto:

1. To us art is an adventure into an unknown world, which can be explored only by those willing to take the risks.
2. This world of imagination is fancy-free and violently opposed to common sense.
3. It is our function as artists to make the spectator see the world our way—not his way.
4. We favor the simple expression of the complex thought. We are for the large shape because it has the impact of the unequivocal. We wish to reassert the picture plane. We are for flat forms because they destroy illusion and reveal truth.
5. It is a widely accepted notion among painters that it does not matter what one paints as long as it is well painted. This is the essence of academism. There is no such thing as good painting about nothing. We assert that the subject is crucial and only that subject-matter is valid which is tragic and timeless. That is why we profess spiritual kinship with primitive and archaic art.

The desire to ignore the individual and achieve the universal was not unique to the modern era, however. Two hundred years prior, painter Sir Joshua Reynolds and author Samuel Johnson proselytized that true art needed to present the general, not the specific; the elevated, not the localized. They believed it was the artist's responsibility to correct and compensate for man's imperfection. The artistic milieu at the time considered the depictions of rural peasants and craggy rocks too garish, if not outright vulgar.

But unlike Reynolds and Johnson, who labored to elevate their subject to a kind of platonic ideal, the avant-garde of modern artists moved away from the actual and individual, not by elevating their subject but by obliterating it, leaving behind only emotion and viscera.

# CALIFORNIA COOL

Don Draper understands Los Angeles. Beyond the Edenic weather and low-slung subdivisions, Don says—without irony—to a would-be client that in California, "Everything is new, and it's clean. The people are filled with hope." If you believe, as I do, in the notion that cities at the epicenter of cultural shifts embody the ethos of their era—for example, Boston embodied the revolutionary spirit of 1776, Chicago was welded together by the industrial revolution, whereas New York was a city that defined the immigrant experience and Victorian values—then no other city in the country is more representative of twentieth-century modernism than Los Angeles.

Los Angeles is where the oppressive caste system of gray, dense, Eastern cities could be cast off and the promise of home ownership could be fulfilled. Whether this experiment was a success is debatable, but this is, at least, the story Los Angeles tells itself—and it is a story that has been believed. It is a magnificent pitch.

It is a city defined by the cars, space, celluloid, and hypnotic rhythms of the Endless Summer.

Like Don's bungalow in Long Beach, Southern California offered the highest possible life for the middle classes: a small but airy home with an open yard that allowed the resident to move fluidly between den and patio. Where our continent stopped, there you could find a homestead replete with whooshing freeways, public beaches, and platoons of bronze-tinged California Girls.

Everything is new in Los Angeles because everything actually *is* new. It is a city obsessed with surface, from architecture to culture: Newness is the lifeblood of Los Angeles. When something gets old we tear it down. History is disposable in Los Angeles; it's the poetry of constant reinvention that speaks to Dick Whitman.

In Palm Springs, we never learn the full names or identities of the Fellini-esque aristocrats with whom Don escapes. Names like Rockefeller, Astor, Rothschild, Dykeman—or Whitman—mean nothing in the desert. The whole scene is drenched in a democracy of the sun. Nothing has come before and few think of tomorrow. As Las Vegas would later be called, Southern California in 1962 was the epicenter of the Eternal Now. In their horizontal mansion they idle in concrete splendor and anonymity. The mansion itself is a triumph of modernism: horizontal, cool, open.

Waist-deep, arms outstretched, facing the abyss, Don submerges himself in the Pacific Ocean. Like the American in the 1960s, Don meets himself in the West.

# CONRAD HILTON: **COLD WARRIOR**

Conrad Hilton single-handedly beat back communism. Well, that's what he joked to a *Time* magazine reporter in 1963. One of the main reasons Hilton was able to become the head of the innkeeping empire was because his chain built clean, efficient hotels in developing countries where people could meet and, per Hilton, "get along with each other."

Hilton was willing to lose some initial profit to gain a foothold into new markets:

> "We think we are helping out in the struggle that is going on in the cold war today with world travel," says Hilton. "These hotels are examples of free enterprise that the Communists hate to see." He likes to say that "we beat Communism into the Caribbean by ten years," and one of his top financial backers, Henry Crown, adds: "We're second only to the Peace Corps."[1]

In his 1957 autobiography, *Be My Guest,* about the ethos of the Hilton brand in far-off lands, Hilton wrote that each of his international hotels was "a little America," a "laboratory" where foreign guests could "inspect America and its ways at their leisure."

But Connie, as he asked his friends to call him, was also a success due to his folksy charm and surprising naiveté. He was quick to respond to inquiries put out by podunk tourism ministers and would close the deal with face-to-face meetings. From *Time* again:

---

1. "Hotels: By Golly!" *Time*, July 19, 1963.

The surprise about Hilton is that he is so much like the guests he caters to. Boyish, candid, trusting, he never fails to be amazed and pleased—even astonished—by the world around him. He cannot get over the speed of jet planes or his possession of a $100 Texas-style Stetson, whose price he mentions to anyone who will listen. He is susceptible to even the most transparent flattery.

Hilton's overseas hotels were also designed to be the place where the Pete and Trudy Campbells of the world would feel comfortable. They were places for rich Americans who wanted to dip a toe into postwar Europe without sacrificing the protective comforts of Westchester.

While it is easy to look down on vanilla products like the Hilton, their real value (as with McDonald's) is vastly improved efficiency and product consistency, which flattened local boutique competition. While fancy Euro-brands could be more sensitive to local character (Lane Pryce could adapt to New York and Bombay, while Hilton's middle-American style was totally obtuse), they were utterly incapable of producing cheap, reliable, mass-market products.

This could help explain Conrad's vision for Moon hotels that he shares with Don. If men were going to be able to travel to the most terrifying unknown frontiers, shouldn't they be greeted with clean towels and complimentary soap and shampoo?

# KHRUSHCHEV BARRED FROM TOMORROWLAND

*After all the things we threw at Khrushchev, you know what made him fall apart? He couldn't get into Disneyland.*

—CONRAD HILTON

The Russians! They can be so problematic to the likes of cold warriors like Conrad Hilton. Like shoe-banger[1] Nikita Khrushchev, who threw a tantrum when he was barred[2] from visiting Disneyland on a meet-and-greet excursion to the States. This snub, according to capitalist stalwart Hilton, is what cinched our victory in the cold war.

During the diplomatically fraught visit in 1959, Khrushchev announced that he wanted to spend some time in Anaheim's Magic Kingdom. Neither the LAPD nor the suits at Disney, they said, could guarantee Khrushchev's safety. So during a dinner hosted by 20th Century-Fox (with Judy Garland, Frank Sinatra, and Marilyn Monroe[3] cavorting around with some Russians from the Politburo), General Secretary Khrushchev was informed that the trip would have to be canceled. Khrushchev, who had already taken a fair amount of razzing from studio heads and senators, was upset by the denial and left Los Angeles the next day.

It's unsurprising that Connie would regard with such pleasure the desires of a wily dictator getting snuffed out by a cartoon mouse. Hilton and Walt Disney shared similar views about their role in

---

1. William Taubman, "Did He Bang It? Nikita Khrushchev and the Shoe," *New York Times*, July 26, 2003.

2. "Premier Annoyed by Ban on a Visit to Disneyland," *New York Times*, September 20, 1959.

3. Peter Carlson, "Nikita Khrushchev Goes to Hollywood," *Smithsonian Magazine*, July 2009.

Soviet Union premier Khrushchev and actress Shirley MacLaine.

American culture. While the rest of the country rumbled with social turmoil, both men believed that their particular blend of folksiness and modern efficiency could secure social harmony. They both built their empires on the notion that respect for traditional values could establish (or reestablish) order among a diverse and unruly public. Conrad's vision for Moon hotels echoes Disney's homespun vision of Tomorrowland: the harrowing solitude of space made orderly, sanitized, and comfortable, with a Bible in every bureau.

# "ONE HELL OF A FOCUS GROUP": THE PORT HURON STATEMENT

When the recently founded and still obscure Students for a Democratic Society declared, "we would replace power rooted in possession, privilege, or circumstance by power and uniqueness rooted in love, reflectiveness, reason, and creativity" during a 1962 convention in Ann Arbor, it certainly would have been aghast to learn that part of its organizing manifesto was used as a way to hawk coffee to young folks.[1]

The twentysomething hipster ad team, Kurt and Smitty, serve as ambassadors from the youth vanguard for Sterling Cooper on the Martinson coffee account. To illustrate the mood and taste of the times, Smitty tells Don about the SDS Port Huron statement (which was sent to him by a friend from Michigan along with a "shitty note" about Smitty's career choice). The actual document rebukes apathy and hypocrisy, and calls for a realignment of top-down institutions and an end to cold war militarism that enabled violence and exploitation abroad. Smitty sums it up like this: "Your generation wants to talk about that newly designed can and the premium beans. But we don't want to be told what we should do *or* how we should act. We just want to be."

While co-opting an indictment of capitalism to pitch coffee to college kids wasn't exactly in the spirit of the Port Huron statement, Kurt and Smitty did present Don with an accurate sense of the ominous mood and aspirations of an emergent counterculture.

To give you a taste for the turbulent times ahead for the men of

---

1. The Port Huron statement was never marketed. It was a mimeographed pamphlet of twenty thousand copies, and sold for thirty-five cents. "We were jaundiced toward the very notion of public relations," said main author and SDS president Tom Hayden in 2002.

Madison Avenue, here's a diagnosis of youth culture from the sixty-four-year-old president of Columbia University, Grayson Kirk. In 1968, as his university was being occupied by the SDS, Kirk said:

> Our young people, in disturbing numbers, appear to reject all forms of authority, from whatever source derived, and they have taken refuge in a turbulent and inchoate nihilism whose sole objectives are destruction. I know of no time in our history when the gap between the generations has been wider or more potentially dangerous.

SDS leader Mark Rudd responded with this:

> We, the young people, whom you so rightly fear, say that the society is sick and you and your capitalism are the sickness. You call for order and respect for authority; we call for justice, freedom, and socialism. There is only one thing left to say. It may sound nihilistic to you, since it is the opening shot in a war of liberation. . . . "Up against the wall, motherfucker, this is a stick-up."

# HELLFIRE: FOUR LITTLE GIRLS

The pastel walls of the Draper home served as usually reliable and impenetrable barricades against most of the ghastly events of the early 1960s, but occasionally the surging tide of history managed to trickle in.

One summer evening while Betty prepped a family dinner, a solemn-looking Carla set the table while a nationally broadcast funeral played over the radio. Fifteen sticks of dynamite had been planted in the basement of the Sixteenth Street Church in Birmingham, Alabama, a common meeting place for black organizers of the civil rights movement. Four young girls, who were in a Sunday school lesson at the time of the blast, Carole Rosamond Robertson (14), Addie Mae Collins (14), Carol Denise McNair (11), and Cynthia Dionne Wesley (14), were killed.

The church's reverend, who was preparing to give a sermon minutes before the explosion ripped through the building, said that it sounded as though "the whole world was shaking." He described that afternoon to a local newspaper:

"I jerked my head, and within seconds, I raised my head, and all around me was so much dust and soot—and glass had fallen, and plaster from the walls and ceiling, and people had begun to move around the building, and it was so smoky in there that some of the people could hardly be identifiable three feet away from me."[1]

Christopher McNair lost his eleven-year-old daughter Denise in the bombing. In an NPR interview on the forty-fifth anniversary of the bombing, McNair recalled the day: "I never did get there. I never did get there. A block away from the church, I saw my wife's cousin, and she told me, come on, go with me. We can't

---

1. Jeff Hansen and John Archibald, "Church Bomb Felt Like 'World Shaking,'" *Birmingham News*, September 15, 1997.

find Denise. And so I moved her over from under the steering wheel, and we drove over to a hospital, and we fumbled around, and we found somebody else who had been in the morgue. And there lay all four of them, there side by side on the table. And Denise was lying out there with a piece of mortar, it looked like a rock, mashed in her head."

There were spontaneous demonstrations of furious grief in the streets of Birmingham that exacerbated the racial animosity in the town. By the next morning another two were dead. Sixteen-year-old Johnny Robinson was shot and killed by police after throwing stones at cars with white people inside. Two teenagers shot a black thirteen-year-old, Virgil Wade, as he rode his bike through their all-white neighborhood.

Three days after the attack, Martin Luther King Jr. delivered the eulogy.

"The death of these little children may lead our whole Southland from the low road of man's inhumanity to man to the high road of peace and brotherhood," King said. "These tragic deaths may lead our nation to substitute an aristocracy of character for an aristocracy of color. The spilled blood of these innocent girls may cause the whole citizenry of Birmingham to transform the negative extremes of a dark past into the positive extremes of a bright future."

Betty, in a seemingly empathetic gesture, informed Carla that she could keep the radio on "your station" as the funeral service murmured into the dining room and Mrs. Draper set the table.

Officers watch President Kennedy's inaugural speech.

# HOW YOU GET YOUR NEWS:
# THE KENNEDY ASSASSINATION

To understand how the stunning news of November 22, 1963, would have reached a young bride sequestered in her hotel room, like Roger's daughter was, or a Sterling Cooper secretary who had her radio off, let's look at the numbers.

Out of a group of 419 people polled ten days after the assassination, the majority reported learning about the shooting from other people—either by phone, from a coworker, or out while shopping or eating. More than half said they learned about it *first* directly from another person.[1]

Nine out of ten respondents who had heard the president had been shot before the announcement that he was dead said they knew about the shooting within forty-five minutes. Their reaction was to then use mass media to confirm what they had heard. Researchers suggested that the data showed that news of immense importance is most likely to be disseminated person to person than less important news. This ran contrary to earlier studies, which suggested mass media disseminated important news faster than interpersonal communication. Which explains the wedding table chatter about "what those phone operators were really up to" when phone lines in entire cities went dead perfectly in step.

Seventy-nine percent of the entire sample surveyed knew about the shooting within forty-five minutes of the first announcement; the last person to hear about the assassination was someone who heard the news three hours later, at 1:30 P.M. Can you imagine what *that* guy's story was? In addition, more respondents said they

---

1. All statistics are taken from Bradley S. Greenberg, "Diffusion of News About the Kennedy Assassination," in *The Kennedy Assassination and American Public: Social Communication and Crisis,* edited by Bradley S. Greenberg and Edwin B. Parker (Stanford, Calif.: Stanford University Press, 1965), 90–94.

learned of the shooting and assassination from the radio rather than the television. This is the breakdown for those people as to how they learned of the shooting before the death announcement was made:

136 people face-to-face
97 from the radio
72 from the television
34 over the telephone

Not to be contrary for the sake of it—because what *can* you say about November 22, 1963, that hasn't already been borrowed three times over?—but the Kennedy family has only limited emotional resonance for those of us born to the baby boomers. This is particularly true for those of us who grew up in the West, far beyond the sway of East Coast political dynasties. Sure, we can identify with the Kennedys as a cultural shift, as style icons, as political talking points. We can also relate to the transformational power of their tragedies—hypnotic television coverage, live carnage, and an unmoored Betty Draper unable to make sense out of any of it. But for us now, that afternoon in Dallas is more illustrative of something else: the swift and unscrupulous pace of history—particularly of recent American history and how it is so phenomenally compressed. In just one generation, the psychic trauma of the assassinations of RFK and JFK has been largely erased. So maybe Don Draper's aloof attitude on that fateful evening is enlightened rather than repressive: "Everything's going to be okay. We have a new president. And we're all going to be sad for a little bit."

# RENO: THE CLEARINGHOUSE OF ILLUSION

A 1934 article on Nevada's divorce law in *Fortune* magazine described the town as "Population 18,500. Elevation 4,500 feet. Reputation: bad."[1] At the turn of the century, divorce laws were so draconian that couples would temporarily migrate to states with looser laws so they could split. States like Arkansas, Wyoming, Idaho, and Nevada lowered their residency requirements to get a chunk of the transient divorce trade. Nevada came out ahead by dropping residency requirements from three months to six weeks. Between 1929 and 1939, more than thirty thousand divorces were granted in Reno.

During the Dust Bowl migration, Nevada locals entered the divorce trade by offering lodging—backrooms, dorms, even private ranches—to couples or stags looking to get their marriage, as they put it in the ads, Reno-vated.

All a disenchanted spouse had to do was book a Reno motel, bide his or her time, and when the forty-second day came, go to a lawyer's office and legally separate from his or her partner who was stationed in some far-flung Eastern city. John Hamlin's *Whirlpool of Reno* described Reno as a "heart-breaking, sophisticated little city—a Monte Carlo of the crude, raw West." The divorce migrants had two main demographics: serious, modest couples; or wives on an errand. According to a 1941 book by journalist Max Miller, divorce was considered women's work. "It is a fact that nine out of ten women who come to Reno for a divorce are doing so under order of their husbands."[2] This spawned an entire genre of movies, journalism, and literature of maudlin plots about women

---

1. "Passion in the Desert," *Fortune* 9, no. 4 (April 1934).

2. Max Miller, *Reno* (New York: Dodd, Mead, 1941), 1.

in the City of Broken Vows. There were stories of newly liberated couples mingling at desert soirees, older women usurped by their husband's young lover, or scared nice girls making "helpless fools of themselves"[3] inside a divorce colony on a terrifying frontier.

---

3. Ibid., 3.

# ACKNOWLEDGMENTS

B ehind this book are three overworked, brilliant women who helped me research, organize, and write—essentially allowing me to bear down on them while I tried to rip this thing out of me: Angela Serratore, Megan Lubaszka, and Natasha Simons. They are extraordinary.

Then there are a few men who inspired me continually to push to produce the best work I possibly could: Choire Sicha, Alex Balk, and David Cho. Choire has served as my chief mentor for the past year. He is a warm center of light I always want to hover around. Alex Balk is the first person who, in his own acerbic way, convinced me that people would want to read something I wrote. He literally helped me to my feet. David Cho, who has a supernatural sense of what's good, ushered this project to a larger audience at *The Awl*.

There's also a league of marvelous professionals who gave me the skills and moxie to take on a project like this: Ben Schwarz, who summoned my sensibilities to the surface and taught me that cultural studies isn't a pursuit to be ashamed of; Murray Roston, for teaching me how to think about literature and art; Eric Avila, who taught me the dynamism of history; and Glenn Gaslin, for plucking me out of the Internet ether and giving me a voice.

The tribe of warrior women, Julia Cheiffetz and Katie Salisbury at HarperCollins and Kate Lee at ICM, whose gumption and dedication made this project possible.

Oodles of gratitude to the contributors whose fabulous work I was introduced to through the magic of the blogosphere: Tim Siedell, Carol Diehl, Dave Wilkie, Angela Natividad, and Bill Green. Thanks to Fred Courtright for wrangling a dizzying amount of copyrights for all the images you see. I'm honored to have had the assistance of Myra Janco Daniels on this project.

My adoration to the remarkable network of friends whose combined support, work, and guidance have kept me afloat: Matt Gallaway, my best friends Ryan Orenstein and Katie Mead, Mary H. K. Choi, Doree Shafrir, Lauren Speer, Michael Adams, Ande Dagan, Cynthia Clarfield, Katie Baker, Julie Klausner, Ryan Ruby, Micah and Lucia, Patrick Saxon, Josh Schein, Molly McAleer, Jim Gibson, Sascha Cohen, and a lady named MathNet.

J. Matthew Cahill is a name I write over and over. I'm not sure what will convince him of the role he continues to play in my life. Hopefully this helps.

It feels a little gauche to thank strangers who share no connection to me, but thanks to Matt Weiner and the writers, designers, and cast of *Mad Men*. Your efforts serve as a constant muse to me. The excellence of your art compels me to do my best at all times. I hope you guys like this!

Then there are the two people I promised I would thank in my Oscar speech—but as the chance of that grows ever more unlikely, I hope this will suffice. Marc Cooper is my dad and the greatest influence on my life. Everything I have ever done is to make him proud. I owe him my talents and vices. Patricia Vargas-Cooper is my best friend and my mother; she taught me how to be a woman. She is a constant source of vitality and love. I owe her my personality, impeccable sense of charm, grace, and modesty.

# ILLUSTRATION CREDITS

| | |
|---|---|
| 97: | Time & Life Pictures/Getty Images |
| 98: | Hulton Archive/Getty Images |
| 103: | Hulton Archive/Getty Images |
| 104: | Midwood |
| 108: | Ballantine Ale |
| 113: | Time & Life Pictures/Getty Images |
| 114: | Bettmann/Corbis |
| 119: | Hulton Archive/Getty Images |
| 122: | Stanford School of Medicine |
| 126: | Time & Life Pictures/Getty Images |
| 131: | Bettmann/Corbis |
| 132: | Super Stock |
| 136: | Drexel Catalogue |
| 140: | Drexel Catalogue |
| 141: | *National Geographic*/Getty Images |
| 143: | Red Cover |
| 144: | Bridgeman Art Library |
| 147: | Library of Congress |
| 148: | Library of Congress |
| 150: | Drexel Catalogue |
| 154: | Original art by Christina Perry and Derrick Gee |
| 157: | Original art by Christina Perry and Derrick Gee |
| 160: | Original art by Christina Perry and Derrick Gee |
| 162: | Original art by Christina Perry and Derrick Gee |
| 165: | Original art by Christina Perry and Derrick Gee |
| 168: | Original art by Christina Perry and Derrick Gee |
| 174: | *Clark Gable, Cary Grant, John Wayne*:Hulton Archive/Getty Images; *Humphrey Bogart*:Time & Life Pictures/Getty Images |
| 179: | Hulton Archive/Getty Images |
| 182: | Hulton Archive/Getty Images |
| 185: | Hulton Archive/Getty Images |
| 186: | Hulton Archive/Getty Images |
| 189: | Ernst Haas/Getty Images |
| 191: | Hulton Archive/Getty Images |
| 194: | Getty Images |
| 198: | K.J. Historical/Corbis |
| 202: | AFP/Getty Images |
| 206: | Time & Life Pictures/Getty Images |
| 209: | Time & Life Pictures/Getty Images |
| 211: | Time & Life Pictures/Getty Images |
| 212: | Redferns |
| 217: | Bettmann/Corbis |
| 218: | Time & Life Pictures/Getty Images |
| 222: | *National Geographic* |
| 232: | Nikola Tamindzic |

# INDEX

# ABOUT THE AUTHOR

---

After graduating from UCLA with a BA in history and working as a union organizer in L.A. and Washington, D.C., for a number of years, Natasha Vargas-Cooper began her writing career as a film critic for *E! Entertainment*. Her reporting, essays, and interviews have appeared in print and Web publications ranging from *The Daily Beast*, *New York*, and *BlackBook* to *Gawker* and *Interview*. She is currently the Los Angeles correspondent for *The Awl*.